THE OLD MAN DIED
(AND HE'S DEAD)

THE OLD MAN DIED
(AND HE'S DEAD)

SIN AND CHRISTIAN RESPONSIBILITY

David A. Swincer

Copyright © 2016 by David A. Swincer, South Australia, Australia. All rights reserved. No part of this book may be used or reproduced in any manner whatsoever without written permission of the publisher, except in the case of brief quotations in articles and reviews.

First edition 2016

MK IV April, 2022

ISBN: 978-0-9808703-5-0

Integrity Publications, South Australia, AUSTRALIA.

Web: www.integritypublications.biz
(Copies of the e-book are available at this website)
(See other titles also)

Email: publications.integrity@gmail.com

ACKNOWLEDGEMENT

Again I offer my sincere thanks to Josh Barrie for the cover design and IT assistance. He is always available and most obliging, and for that I am most grateful.

DEDICATION

To my late friend and mentor, and lecturing colleague, Dr. Ted Gibson.

Ted was a master of independent thinking, coupled with careful research and exhaustive biblical study.

His study on the subject of the Old Man is unique in my experience, and I am greatly indebted to him for this careful research. It is a pity that he did not publish his sound biblical material.

NOTES

1. "Man/him/he" is used in the generic sense throughout this book.

2. Bible references are quoted from the NIV, unless otherwise stated.

3. References are made using the Harvard system, to avoid excessively cumbersome referencing, and to be immediately available for access.

4. Exegetical notes on verses, follow the verses using bullets:
   - "text being addressed"
     - "notes within that text"

5. Having purchased a copy of the book, if you are interested in being able to use a navigation panel for studying and searching, please contact the publisher at the above website and make your request for a free e-copy in Word format. Provide purchase date and details plus "First edition – 2016", MK IV, April 2022.

* * * * *

CONTENTS

FOREWORD XIII
INTRODUCTION 1
CHAPTER 1: REFLECTIONS 5
1.1 Some Questions to Clarify the Foundation 5
1.2 Summary And Conclusion From The First Volume 10
1.3 Consequences For Me Now That I Am a Sinner 12
1.4 Questions And Ramifications for This Volume 12
1.5 Passing the Buck. 13
CHAPTER 2: THE NATURE OF SIN 15
2.1 Definition of sin 15
2.2 Motivation for Sin: Operation of the Will. 23
   2.2.1 The will: Positive Operation 24
   2.2.2 The will: Neutral Operation 27
   2.2.3 The will: Negative Operation—by-passed 30
2.3 The Flesh (not "nature") 45
   2.3.1 Introduction 47
   2.3.2 Examples of the Flesh—Objectively 57
   2.3.3 Brief Scrutiny of Galatians 5. 62
2.4 Learned Behaviour (as a Christian) 76
CHAPTER 3: THE OLD MAN 79
3.1 Introduction 79
3.2 The Old Man—in Three Passages 80
   3.2.1 ROMANS 6:6 80
   3.2.2 EPHESIANS 4:21-22 83
   3.2.3 COLOSSIANS 3:9 85
3.3 The New Man—in Three Passages 86
   3.3.1 Introduction 86
   3.3.2 Note: the Transition: Old →New 87
   3.3.3 Looking at the New Man in the Three Passages 91
      A. Romans 6. 91

    B. Ephesians 4:23-27 92
    C. Colossians 3: 7-8, 10 92
  3.4 Translations of Old/New Man 93
    3.4.1 Old Man 93
    3.4.2 New Man 95
    3.4.3 Warning 95

CHAPTER 4: CULPABILITY FOR SIN 99
4.1 Introduction 99
4.2 Three Categories of Sin 99
  4.2.1 Deliberate Sins 100
  4.2.2 Unintentional Or Unwitting Sins 101
  4.2.3 Habit Sins... 102
  4.2.4 Resolution Of Habit Sins 104
4.3 Culpability In All Situations 104

CHAPTER 5: LIFE UNDER THE NEW MAN 107
5.1 Introduction 107
5.2 Mastery of Sin Removed 109
5.3 Freedom Not to Sin: The Consenting Will 110
5.4 Life Under Grace 113
  5.4.1 Romans 6 (and following). 114
  5.4.2 Ephesians 4 (and following). 116
  5.4.3 Colossians 3 (and following). 119
  5.4.4 Mortifying the Habits/Practices. 121
5.5 How To Deal With Sin—In The Three Categories 121
  5.5.1 Introduction: Common Ground 121
    1) The Will—The Operation of the Consenting Will. 122
    2) Attitude of the Mind. 126
    3) Accountability... 143
  5.5.2 Comments On Each Of The Three Categories Of Sin 145
    1) Deliberate Sin 145
    2) Unwitting Sin.. 148
    3) Habit Sin 148

CHAPTER 6: CONCLUSIONS 155
6.1 The Old Man is Dead 155
6.2 Clarify the Terms... 155

6.3 The New Man. 155
6.4 Inculcated Habits. 155
6.5 Devotional Life. 156
6.6 Accepting Responsibility. 156
BIBLIOGRAPHY 157
APPENDIX: MY GRANDFATHER'S CLOCK 161
BIOGRAPHICAL SKETCH 165
FURTHER READING 167

* * * * *

FOREWORD

"It's all Adam's fault!"

OK. Then you have just condemned yourself to a Christless eternity!

Reflect carefully on the statement just made.

In an earlier volume on the doctrine of original sin: *Condemned Already*, we noted, that if Adam is to be blamed for **our** condemnation, then we have to address the reason for **his** condemnation. Adam was innocent until he sinned in regard to the prohibition of the Tree of Life. At that point he "died". Spiritually he was cut-off and alienated from God and out of fellowship, and God immediately announced His already-prepared plan of rescue. The Son of the descendant of the woman (Eve)—the Lord Jesus Christ—would bruise the serpent's head (the serpent who was the vehicle for Adam's sin and fall through the temptation orchestrated by Satan):

> *[15] And I will put enmity between you and the woman, and between your offspring and hers; he will crush your head, and you will strike his heel."*
>
> Genesis 3:15.

The situation for Adam is clear enough. He was innocent, and then became a sinner, by sinning. We can easily identify the CAUSATIVE sin that was responsible for his demise—his default in regard to the Tree of Life.

> *[16] And the Lord God commanded the man, "You are free to eat from any tree in the garden; [17] but **you must not eat from the tree of the knowledge of good and evil, for when you eat from it you will certainly die."***
>
> Genesis 2:16-17, emphasis added.

At the point of his sin—eating from the Tree of Life—he "died". Spiritually he was cut-off from God. Physical death came later.

But if Adam's sin is the CAUSATIVE sin that constitutes *me* a sinner—and that is the majority view—then I am condemned to a Christless eternity, all because of Adam's sin.

Supposedly in solidarity with the human race, every man woman and child of all time is condemned—not on his own account—but because of Alien Guilt inherited from Adam.

Adam's sin is thus my sin.

The tragedy is, if Adam's sin **IS** CAUSATIVE for me (but I don't believe that it is) and for my condemnation (*Condemned Already*), then the only way that I can reverse that situation is to address the CAUSATIVE sin. **But it is not my sin!** And I can't repent of another person's sin. I can't repent of Adam's sin. I can't address the foundational issue. So I can't address the cause of my condemnation, and therefore I can't be saved!

The seriousness of this situation seems to escape most theologians. Why? **This is serious.**

This critical issue was the basis of that first volume, and was the central issue that was addressed, demonstrating that we are each personally CULPABLE and responsible to God for our sin—the CAUSATIVE sin that constituted EACH of us as a sinner. And hence we are condemned JUSTLY and PERSONALLY.

All people of all time are individually responsible for their own sin and hence of their condemnation. That being the case, they can—indeed MUST—repent of **their own sin** in order to be saved.

Thus God is just in His demands and fair in his expectations based upon the finished work of Christ.

We now move on to the next step—the role of the Christian in terms of his individual accountability and culpability for his own sins **as a Christian**.

* * * * *

INTRODUCTION

My grandfather's clock
Was too large for the shelf,
So it stood ninety years on the floor;
It was taller by half
Than the old man himself,
Though it weighed not a pennyweight more.
It was bought on the morn
Of the day that he was born,
It was always his treasure and pride;
**But it stopped short
Never to go again,
When the old man died.**

I was always impressed by the words in bold type (added), of this verse from the poem *My Grandfather's Clock* by Henry Clay Work (Copyright Unknown). It seemed to convey a "heavy" theology that most Christians missed—although of course it was not addressing anything remotely like a theological issue! (See Appendix, for the complete poem).

The Bible says:

*[6]Knowing this, that **our old man is crucified with him**, that the body of sin might be destroyed, that henceforth we should not serve sin.*

Romans 6:6 (emphasis added).

As far as the Christian is concerned, "The Old Man died, never to rise again". The Old Man is dead!

And yet I repeatedly hear people excusing themselves for their sin, because, "The Old Man affected me and compelled me". Or more commonly, they use the term "the sin nature". "I was influenced by my sin nature/old nature". See extra discussion on the Natures in Chapter 2.

It's not my fault!!

- As a *non-Christian*, we could blame Adam for making me a sinner.
- Now as a *Christian*, who do I blame for my daily sins? The Old Man?

We just don't want to accept responsibility for our actions.

The first volume—*Condemned Already*—addressed our culpability for our CAUSATIVE sin. The sin that constituted me a sinner in the first place.

This volume addresses our culpability for our sin as a Christian. We need to start our search here at precisely this point, a careful exegesis of the biblical teaching concerning **the Old Man.**

There are five pivotal issues to be dealt with.

There is no particular order or progression, and the five are variously interrelated, but they are essential in attempting to understand this issue of the Christian responsibility and accountability for his sin. These issues are:

1. The will and sin.

It is imperative to note the direct relationship between the will and sin. There is no place for some independent third party to force our hand to sin. Nor is our will pre-programmed or pre-conditioned or biased.

2. The by-passed will.

It is the failure to identify this factor—as an extension of the issue of the will—that has led to so much angst in trying to rationalise Romans 7 and the "wretched man".

3. The flesh.

The inaccurate translations that consistently change the very simple word "flesh" and transform it into some type of independent personality with determinative powers, that makes a mockery of Scripture and confuses the whole issue—or at least inhibits it from coming to a biblical conclusion.

4. The flesh, especially in Galatians 5.

The application of the issue of the flesh in the particular context of Galatians 5—as if it were this independent person—is very significant in the restrictions it places upon a balanced view of the biblical position concerning the Christian walk as a tension between the natural desires of the normal human being, and the new values of the fruit of the Spirit.

5. The Old Man.

Again, it is a less than adequate translation problem that has initiated and then perpetuated a whole range of misunderstandings in regard to the Christian position, standing and walk.

But first of all, let us ask questions that will sharpen the focus of the questions for both areas—responsibility for sinning in order to become a sinner, and responsibility for sinning as a Christian—in order to gain a better perspective.

* * * * *

CHAPTER 1

REFLECTIONS

GAINING PERSPECTIVE

[18]Whoever believes in him is not condemned, but whoever does not believe stands **condemned already** *because he has not believed in the name of God's one and only Son.*

John 3:18, emphasis added.

1.1 SOME QUESTIONS TO CLARIFY THE FOUNDATION (FROM THE FIRST VOLUME: *CONDEMNED ALREADY*).

1.1.1 Am I condemned:

    a. because I am a sinner, or

    b. because I sinned, or

    c. because I refuse to believe?

1.1.2 If #1.1.1-a, then did I *become* a sinner (the CAUSATIVE sin):

    a. because Adam sinned, giving a "sinful bias" to the human race (hereditary depravity), or

    b. because I simply descended from Adam (seminal identity, "condemnation by generation"), or

    c. because of both the above (representative view), or

d. because of cumulative degeneration (cf. Romans 1:24-32), or

e. because I independently chose to sin ("everyone his own Adam", neo-orthodoxy or Pelagianism), or

f. because as a free agent I imitated (mimicked) Adam (Pelagianism), or

g. because I individually and responsibly sinned in Adam? [cf. #1.1.1-b], or

h. because I "arrived at moral consciousness" (Strong 1907, 573)? or

i. because I was born with a "corrupt nature"? etc.

NOTE: a CAUSATIVE sin, is the sin that constitutes me a sinner, as opposed to being innocent. For Adam this was the taking of the fruit from the Tree of the Knowledge of Good and Evil. But how did **I** become a sinner? **What** was **my** CAUSATIVE sin? **When** was it?

NOTE: #1.1.1-c is not CAUSATIVE, but the reason that I might *continue (remain)* in a state of condemnation, as John 3:36 indicates (emphasis added):

*36Whoever believes in the Son has eternal life, but whoever rejects the Son will not see life, for **God's wrath remains on him**."*

1.1.3 For *whose* sin am I condemned:
a. for Adam's sin, or

b. for my sin?

1.1.4 If I am condemned for Adam's sin (#1.1.3-a):
a. How do I relate to Romans 5:12 (emphasis added)?

> [12]*Therefore, just as sin entered the world through one man, and death through sin, and in this way **death came to all men, BECAUSE ALL SINNED**—*

According to this verse, death passed to all men, **not** because Adam sinned and thus affected all men, not because I was simply "born", not because I inherited some "sin nature" or a "bias", but because **all sinned. Every man individually sinned**.

b. How do I relate to Romans 3:23 (emphasis added)?

> [23]*for **all have sinned** and fall short of the glory of God.*

If I am counselling a person to Christ, do I quote this verse to indicate that he needs to repent of **his own** sin, but then tell him that that is not really true, because it was actually Adam's sin!?

c. How do I address Ezekiel's assertion that sin is a *personal* responsibility:

> [20]*The **soul who sins is the one who will die**. The son will not share the guilt of the father, nor will the father share the guilt of the son. ...*
>
> Ezekiel 18:20, emphasis added.

d. How do I respond to Moses' statement:

> [16]*Fathers shall not be put to death for their children, nor children put to death for their fathers; **each is to die for his own sin.***
>
> Deuteronomy 24:16, emphasis added.

1.1.5 If Adam is responsible:

If Adam is responsible for the sin that condemns *me*, and by extension is responsible for the sin that condemns *all* men, then would not Christ's death atone for Adam's sin and thereby redeem all? (Universalism). It CANNOT be both ways. If the

one sin that supposedly affected all men of all time (automatically, procreationally, etc.), is atoned for by the **one** death of Christ on the cross, then surely all men must be redeemed, automatically.

1.1.6 If #1.1.5 is not true:

(and it is not), but since Adam's **causative sin** must necessarily be the object of Christ's death, then it must follow that only Adam has been saved. How do we now explain the salvation for all mankind?

1.1.7 If I am condemned for *my* sin (#1.1.3-b):
a. could I therefore die for **my** sin?
b. could any other person die for me?
c. did Christ die for me?

1.1.8 If Christ died for me (#1.1.7-c), who died for you?

As a matter of justice, how could Christ die for more than one sin, or more than one person? ("If Christ died for me, who died for you?") And if He died for ONE sin, which sin was that? (See "The Law of Multiplying Returns" in *Condemned Already*, Swincer 2011a, #4.6).

1.1.9 The justice of God

If God is just (and I firmly believe that He is), would He condemn me for another's (Adam's) sin?

We have noted this serious problem previously:

History has recorded the persistent revulsion many have felt at the apparent impropriety of being divinely condemned for an occurrence prior to their birth and for which they made no conscious choice. (Otto 1990, 205).

> I agree with Guthrie (1981, 212), as he refers to Romans 5:12, that "Paul's whole approach to the subject of sin elsewhere would **not support the view that any man is held responsible for the sinful bias** (sic) **he has inherited**" (emphasis added).
>
> The focus of the debate in the doctrine of original sin is on the joint issues of **alien guilt** and **the justice of God**.

Two questions demand answer, first, how we can be responsible for a depraved nature (sic) which we did not personally and consciously originate; and, secondly, how God can justly charge to our account the sin of the first father of the race [alien guilt].

Strong 1907, 593.

I do not think the doctrine of the Fall can be used to show that it is "just", in terms of retributive justice, to punish individuals for the faults of their remote ancestors.

Lewis 1940, 58.

> Hence the conclusion is: *Condemned Already.*

1.1.10 *For what* did Christ die?

a. Adam's sin, or
b. my sin, or
c. your sin, or
d. sin**s** (plural—cumulatively all the sins of all people of all time)—this would eliminate "limited atonement", or
e. sin (as a principle), or
f. all the people of the world, or … ?

1.2 SUMMARY AND CONCLUSION FROM THE FIRST VOLUME (#1.1 above):

1.2.1 I am responsible for *my* sin (not Adam's).

*^{12}All have turned away, they have together become worthless; there is **no one** who **does good**, not even one."*

Romans 3:12, emphases added.

*^{23}for **all have sinned** and fall short of the glory of God,*

Romans 3:23, emphasis added.

NOTE: Romans 3:23, indicates a CAUSATIVE sin. It is the sin that results in "falling short of God's glory". This is the sin that CAUSES **me to become a sinner who is condemned. But **when, where**, and **why** did this happen?

1.2.2 I am justly condemned for *my* sin, alone.

*^{12}Therefore, just as sin entered the world through one man, and death through sin, and in this way death came to all men, **because all sinned*** (Romans 5:12, emphasis added).

1.2.3 Only Christ could have died for me
(and indeed for any sin):

^{8}... While we were still sinners, Christ died for us.

Romans 5:8.

1.2.4 I sinned personally:

but we **all** sinned **personally, corporately** and **responsibly** in Adam. This is the **faith identification position** (Swincer 2011a, *Condemned Already*). This is understood by IDENTIFICATION with the two Adam's, and apprehended by faith:

*^{22}For **as in Adam** all die, **so in Christ** all will be made alive.* (1 Corinthians 15:22, emphases added).

BY FAITH I understand that I sinned in Adam (*in Adam all die*)—a **corporate identity** act. (cf. 1.1.2-g, above).

**THIS IS MY CAUSATIVE SIN.

BY FAITH I understand that I am crucified in Christ (*in Christ all will be made alive*)—a **corporate identity** act, leading to new life in Him.

Further, in this corporate identity with Christ:

[5]*If we have been **united with him** like this in his death*
...
[6]*For we know that **our old (man) was crucified with him** so that the body of sin might be done away with, that we should no longer be slaves to sin*

                      Romans 6:5, 6, emphases added.

The corporate identity is clearly emphasized. "We" and "our" are used, and the latter is of special significance since it—as a *plural*—is linked with "man' which is *singular*. Thus there is a singular/corporate act that is referred to. There is an *individual* but *corporate* responsibility.

1.2.5 We thus conclude:

that there is ONE corporate death in Christ, and following from the comparison in 1 Corinthians 15:22 (above), there is ONE corporate sin in Adam.

1.2.6 Since there is therefore only ONE sin:

then Christ needs to die only ONE death, paying the penalty for that ONE sin, and thus atoning for all mankind with perfect justice.

(See *Condemned Already,* Swincer 2011a, for the development of this thesis).

1.2.7 I am now a sinner, on my own account. It is my fault.

1.3 CONSEQUENCES FOR ME NOW THAT I AM A SINNER.

As a sinner, it is natural for me to sin.

A cow moos because it is a cow.

A dog barks because it is a dog.

A sinner sins because he is a sinner.

BUT a cow does not have to **always** moo.

A dog doesn't have to **always** bark (although some seem to have not gotten that message!).

And a sinner does not have to **always** sin. It is a choice.

**NOTE: I sinned and therefore became a sinner. I now sin because (although without compulsion) I am a sinner. It is natural to me. And it is easy to sin.

But what happens to me when I become a Christian? I have to address my responsibility as **a saved sinner. This is the focus of this volume.**

1.4 QUESTIONS AND RAMIFICATIONS FOR THIS VOLUME.

1.4.1 As opposed to my status as a non-Christian:
as a Christian, why do I sin:
a. because I want to, or
b. because I can't help it, or
c. because I am compelled to?

1.4.2 If the answer is "a":

then I am indicating that this is a personal choice. I confirm that I don't have to sin. I confirm that I deliberately sin. Shame!!

1.4.3 I nevertheless also confirm that:

even as a Christian, I am still a sinner—but now a saved sinner. And there are other areas besides deliberate sin that are the cause of much tension and stress.

1.5 PASSING THE BUCK.

There are TWO major areas being addressed here.

A. The CAUSATIVE sin (singular) whereby I become and am constituted a sinner,

B. The sins (plural) that I commit as a sinner, especially after becoming a Christian.

In both these areas, the common tendency is to "pass the buck".

A. If it is the CAUSATIVE sin, the tendency—aided and abetted by theologians—is that it is Adam's fault rather than mine.

B. If it is my response as a saved sinner, then the tendency is to blame my Old Man. Although, erroneously this is often referred to as a "sin nature". When I become a Christian, a new and very important change occurs, and makes sin more difficult in some ways, but a greater challenge in others. Now I am committed to a new master. See below.

NOTE: The New Testament does not speak in terms of a Christian having *two natures*, one old and the other new. It distinctly uses the word **man (or in other places, flesh). We can refer to a similarity with Christ in that we have a human nature and a divine nature—but not in the sense of a nature as some part of us. The Greek word is used in the sense of "a pleasant nature", "… it is a word which refers to the inherent or essential qualities of any substance or entity", but not as a self-determining entity. Jesus does not have a human and divine nature as parts of Him (cf. the belaboured attempts of the Definition of Chalcedon and the Westminster Confession to try to address this difficulty). He **is** man, and He **is** God (divine)—they are realities of His **being**, not parts of Him, where He is somehow a third party. These concepts should clarify as we proceed.

* * * * *

CHAPTER 2

THE NATURE OF SIN

Against the background assumption of "Passing the Buck", it must be stated that sin comes in three basic forms.

1. Deliberate sin.
2. Subconscious/unconscious sin. Unwitting sin.
3. Habit sin.

It is in the area of "habit sin" that the most controversial issues arise. This is the area that is usually explained away as being caused by the "sin nature", or the more correct term (although not the correct reasoning), "the old man". The area of "passing the buck".

In preparation to examine this, let us look at the issue of sin from a biblical perspective.

2.1 DEFINITION OF SIN.

Sin is fundamentally **an attitude of the mind**. It is this attitude that leads to and results in sin. And it is **always active**—never an inert quantity or commodity.

2.1.1 Sin is anything not of faith.

Romans 14:23 (emphasis added):

[23]... *everything that does not come from faith is sin.*

The focus here is *faith*. Sometimes the root of the word, helps to explain its meaning. If we were to look at the word "faith": *pistis* (πιστις), it is not a word for "blind belief". Primarily it means "firm persuasion", a conviction based upon hearing. The corresponding verb *peithō*, the root verb for *pistis,* means "to persuade", and emphasizes this aspect—persuasion. Romans 4:20-21, referring to Abraham, highlights this meaning (emphases added):

> [20]*Yet he did not waver through unbelief regarding the promise of God, but was* **strengthened in his faith** *and gave glory to God*
> [21]**being fully persuaded** *that God had power to do what he had promised.*

Abraham took no blind leap in the dark. Propositionally he came to the firm **persuasion** that God—being Who He is—will enact precisely what He promised.

When we **refuse to be persuaded** of God, we try to be independent, and like Adam, we want to be "as God".

The Holy Spirit will bring conviction in regard to this refusal to trust God:

> [8]*When he comes, he will* **convict the world** *of guilt in regard to sin ...:*
> [9]*in regard to sin,* **because men do not believe** *(are not persuaded)* **in me;**
>
> John 16:9, emphases added.

It is fundamental to being human to "trust"—to be dependent—on God. To be persuaded of God. Sin is a **refusal** to accept our creatureliness that involves complete dependence upon God. Bultmann says, "denial of God means failure to acknowledge one's own creatureliness" (1952, 232). It is an "irrational assertion of one's own self-dependence **in the presence of God**" (Gibson n.d., 2, emphasis added). It is a shocking fact that this refusal to believe, is not done in isolation, but *in the very presence of God*. It is the height of rudeness to say the least.

This fundamental requirement of being human—to trust—was also manifested in Jesus, the God-Man. Before He could perform His public ministry He had to be tested at the level of His manhood. Would He **trust** God His Father? Was He truly a man Who could die for men? The temptations did not include a question about whether He could turn stones into bread—of course He could, He made the whole universe!—but would He **trust** God having been expressly *led by the Spirit into the desert to be tempted by the devil* (Matthew 4:1). Jesus chose to trust His Father, proving His obedience and thus "qualifying" as our Saviour:

*⁸Although he was a son, **he learned obedience** from what he suffered*
*⁹and, **once made perfect** [as a result of the testing], he became the source of eternal salvation for all who obey him*

Hebrews 5:8, 9, emphases added.

God made Adam in His image, with the ability to make choices and to relate to Him. We have noted that fundamental to this relationship was **trust**, the creature dependent on the Creator. The opportunity to develop this choice-relationship was provided by the prohibition God placed on the Tree of the Knowledge of Good and Evil (Genesis 2:16, 17). Adam had everything to meet his needs, and needed nothing more, and hence the prohibited tree focused on whether God should be trusted and His prohibition respected. Subsequently (Genesis 2:21, 22), Eve was created and no doubt received the information about the tree from her husband. For her it was second-hand information.

Satan tempted Eve to abrogate her dependence on her husband, and through him, her dependence on God, by questioning God's integrity. Eve, who was *in the presence of both God and her husband* ("with her" – Genesis 3:6e), ignored both and violated the trust placed in her. This was a foolish choice—to ignore both God and Adam—and in their very presence—but it was not an act of disobedience that revealed "a will thoroughly corrupted and alienated from God" (Strong 1907, 590). The will itself is not a moral agent, and it is this erroneous theological concept of a corrupted will that supposedly forces the hand of man, thus removing culpability, that was a corrective focus of the earlier book, *Condemned Already* (Swincer, 2011a). The will is neutral, operating on the evidence.

Prior to this point, Eve was not a sinner. She was not yet alienated from God.

The dramatic construct of Eve's choice **in the presence** of God **and** Adam, highlights the horrific and insulting nature of her action. It can be compared to Paul's denunciation of the Gentiles, when they made a choice between "the creature **alongside** the Creator" (Romans 1:25) and insulted the Creator, deliberately choosing the creature, **in the very presence** of the Creator! Eve was thus deceived (1 Timothy 2:14), ignoring both her husband and God. **Eve sinned and therefore became a sinner – before Adam sinned!!**

This was an irrational assertion of self-dependence, with aspirations to divine prerogatives. It smacks of idolatry—noted below.

Subsequently (but almost immediately) Eve introduced the fruit to Adam, but he was in no doubt. He was not deceived (1 Timothy 2:14). He had received the prohibition directly from God prior to the creation of Eve (Genesis. 2:16, 17), so there was no doubt in his mind about his choice to eat, and what God had told him. Eve failed, in that **in the presence of Adam**, who was the mediator of the prohibition, she did not defer to him, not as an inferior (or superior), but as a *created complement and dependent*. Adam failed directly in the sight of God, because he did not exercise his relationship to his **Head**—in Whose very presence he stood—about an issue in which there was no doubt.

He also failed in that he did not protect his wife in her action, of which he was patently aware.

Lack of faith in behaviour is the cause of sin (²³... ***everything that does not come from faith is sin***. Romans 14:23), but the counterpart is also true, that failure to show faith toward **God in Himself**, is displeasing to Him:

> ⁶And ***without faith it is impossible to please God***, because anyone who comes to him ***must believe*** that he exists and that he rewards those who earnestly seek him.
>
> Hebrews 11:6, emphases added.

- "exists": *estin* (ἐστιν) is the third person singular present indicative of the "verb to be": *eimi* (εἰμι). This translation—*exists*—actually misses the point of the verse and the statement. It is not so much a matter of existence as **being**. Where there is no object for the subject (God), then the verb to "be" is reflexive back onto the subject. Hence in the absence of an object in this phrase, the phrase really becomes, "must believe that God is God"—that God is who He claims to be, as distinct from the fact of His existence. Or as the Tetragrammaton (YHWH) implies: "I am Who I am" and "I will be Who I will be". God is Who He is and no one can say otherwise. In order to be pleasing to God, we must believe—be persuaded—that God is Who He claims to be. That we can *trust* Him completely as Abraham did. (See further on the verb "to be" and the Tetragrammaton in Swincer 2019, #1.1).

Faith is our creational relationship with God that recognises our dependence on Him. The refusal to **trust** Him—sin—led to spiritual death. This was a questioning of God's own claim to WHO He is.

Lack of faith led to sin and alienation from God. The way back to God is **through faith** in the work of Jesus, appropriating the death of the Old Man, and the putting on of the

New Man. And in the New Man status, there needs to be continuing **faith**—*being persuaded of God* in all our activities. See below under Chapter 5: LIFE UNDER THE NEW MAN.

This attitude of "refusal to believe" (sin), also has an aspect of rebellion against God, and this is highlighted in the second aspect defining sin.

2.1.2 Sin is lawlessness.

1 John 3:4 (emphasis added):

[4]Everyone who sins breaks the law; in fact, ***sin is lawlessness****.*

The reciprocal is also true: ***lawlessness is sin***

This position is one of opposition to the law. Rebellion against the idea of being restrained. Fundamentally an **attitude**.

David admitted this attitude:

[3]For I know my transgressions [rebellion], *and my sin is always before me.*

Psalm 51:3.

James points out that there is something inclusive about the law:

[10]For whoever keeps the whole law and yet stumbles at just one point is ***guilty of breaking all of it****.*

James 2:10, emphasis added.

The fundamental **attitude** that is prepared to break the law at any point, is the same attitude that will allow breaking the law at any, and every, point. And this is wider than just the Mosaic Law.

Whenever we throw off restraint and become master of our own destiny—which we do—then we have an attitude of lawlessness. We will not be restrained. Nobody will tell us what to do!

All laws require the willing submission—in the first instance—of the subjects to obey those laws. It matters not whether it is quietness in a library, to speeding on the highway (or anywhere else for that matter!), to failing to submit a tax return, or committing murder. And if there is not a willingness to fulfil the obligation, then punishments and coercive measures are usually stipulated to seek to ensure that there is the proper respect for that law or regulation.

This attitude that resists the law, is also rebelliousness.

2.1.3 Sin is rebellion—idolatry.

Sin is active rebellion/disobedience, not a passive condition, or a transmitted disease.

1 Samuel 15:23, emphases added:

*²³For **rebellion** is like the sin of divination, and arrogance like the **evil of idolatry**.*

This verse correlates rebellion with idolatry.

Again the emphasis is clear. The attitude of rebellion and refusal to believe—as in the first two verses we looked at to define sin—is premised on the elevation of the self. This is worship of the self. It is idolatry. Sin is idolatry. When Eve sought to "be as God" her action was idolatry.

Whenever we exalt self over God, we sin. When we pursue those goals that seek to promote only ourselves, it is sin. And it is rebellion against the law and the lawgiver. This is especially noted in the context of the Jewish background. The basic desire of the Jew was to be "righteous", i.e. "in the right".

² "Truly I know that it is so:
*But how can a man be **in the right before God**?*

Job 9:2, ESV, emphasis added.

To be *right with God* required keeping His laws and statutes with all the heart, mind, body, and soul. To fail to do that was rebellion.

NOTE: in each of these three cases, **sin is the result of an operation of the will. It is always active, never an inert commodity. This needs to be emphasised in the context of concepts that speak of "sinful bias", "sinful nature", and other explanations that avoid the will, and therefore *avoid culpability and responsibility for sin.*

The Bible does not speak of bias, compulsion, inclination, or a controlling nature. It speaks of **choice**, and the **will**. We are **beings**, not persons with attached "nature(s)". And fundamental to those unified beings (flesh/body, mind, and emotions) is the responsible action of the will leading to behaviour.

It is somewhat astounding to find that a leading figure like Dr Martyn Lloyd-Jones adopts a view of sin that gives it independent existence as an entity, that subsequently allows for concepts of "natures" that also have independent existence and determinative powers apart from a man. He says:

> … sin is something which is outside man, **something which can exist and which did exist apart from man**. It is something which has entered the human race from without … We are aware of a power other than ourselves acting upon us, and influencing us … But it is not enough to say that **sin is a power which has independent existence** … it is a power which man has allowed to enter his life and which affects him profoundly and vitally.
>
> Lloyd-Jones 1942, 46, emphases added.

This view fails to recognise that sin is not an entity at all, that it does not have independent existence, and that it is related to acts of rebellion. Again, it is the view of a revered Bible teacher that can be responsible for giving currency to an idea that is not substantiated scripturally, that can cause long-term problems theologically.

2.2 MOTIVATION FOR SIN: OPERATION OF THE WILL.

NOTE: **PIVOTAL ISSUE #1: THE WILL AND SIN (See the Introduction).

NOTE: the **will of the ego (self) is the focal point for all sin.

Man has been made in the likeness of God, and as such, *inter alia,* he may choose to be self-loving or self-giving. We are free to make the choice between these two—but it is a choice, the operation of the will.

It should be remembered that the will is neutral as an entity. It is not corruptible. It operates on the evidence available to our minds—which implicates the mind!!

If there is known information, then the will acts **positively**—so #1 below—even if that means that it acts contrary to the information, thus leading to sin. Certainly a choice has been made.

If there is no evidence, the will may be **neutral** in its action (or non-action)—so #2.2.2 below.

If the will has operated (by choice—positively) frequently in a particular direction—for example always eating food—it may result in a conditioning that impinges less and less on the will, ultimately leading to a habit—perhaps gluttony, hence we get #2.2.3. And the will is **by-passed**.

This latter situation was our position as sinners. As sinners we "naturally" sinned, not because we had to, but because it was habitual. We chose NOT to seek God, because

[4]*In his pride the wicked does not seek Him; in all his thoughts there is no room for God,* (Psalm 10:4).

Or as Paul says (Romans 3:11):

¹¹there is no one who understands, no one who seeks God.

The habitual position was to live under the ethos of the Old Man with no reference to God. It was not because there was no knowledge of God, and therefore God held us accountable, because we **did** know the truth:

¹⁸The wrath of God is being revealed from heaven against all the godlessness and wickedness of men who **suppress the truth** *by their wickedness,*
¹⁹since **what may be known about God is plain to them**, *because* **God has made it plain to them**.

Romans 1:18, 19, emphases added.

You cannot suppress what you don't know! Therefore our actions were a betrayal of our knowledge. We had no basis for argument, because God has declared His own revelation, and therefore we were "without excuse":

²⁰For **since the creation** *of the world God's invisible qualities—***his eternal power and divine nature—have been clearly seen**, *being understood from what has been made, so that* **men are without excuse**.

Romans 1:20, emphases added.

This is the pivotal operation in the converted state as well—hence we are **without excuse**—and so we look at the three alternatives for the operation of the will.

2.2.1 The will: POSITIVE OPERATION

As much as we may not wish to admit it, sin is usually the result of a choice! And we WANT to sin! If that is not true, then why do we sin? Most people are ashamed to admit that they deliberately choose to sin, but that is the reality.

**NOTE: *Sin* should not be confused with *temptation*.

> [13] When **tempted**, no one should say, "God is tempting me." For God cannot be tempted by evil, nor does he tempt anyone;
> [14] but each one is tempted when, by his own evil desire, he is dragged away and enticed.
> [15] Then, **after desire has conceived, it gives birth to sin**; and sin, when it is full-grown, gives birth to death.
>
> James 1:14, 15, emphases added.

James makes it very clear that sin results from a person's *willing consent* to yield to temptation. The will is positive. Even being "dragged away and enticed by his own evil desire" is in itself not sin. It is the **yielding to sin**, that is the problem.

Jesus was severely tempted/tested in the wilderness—but that was not sin—and He refused to yield to the temptation however attractive it might be. And we should never underestimate how severe the temptation would have been to avoid separation from His Father—which is what the cross required: "*My God, my God, why have you forsaken me?*" Jesus did not sin because He did not yield, not because He was not tempted or that it was an ineffectual exercise, nor that it was a "cream-puff" exercise.

From the time of Adam, there has been announced a **penalty** for sin—a consequence for the choice to exercise the will in positive rebellion. **Death**—spiritual death initially—is the direct result of sin. It designates alienation from God. Separation from God—never extinction.

> [23] For **the wages of sin is death**, but the gift of God is eternal life in Christ Jesus our Lord.
>
> Romans 6:23, emphasis added.

And Ezekiel clearly asserts the culpability and individual responsibility for the one who makes the choice to sin:

> [4] ... The soul who sins is the one who will die.
> [20] The soul who sins is the one who will die ...
>
> Ezekiel 18:4, 20.

Against the choice to sin, God has always warned that there is a penalty—not the same as the penalty initially to Adam, which was the CAUSATIVE sin leading to condemnation, loss of innocence and the expectation of eternal damnation. But there is always accountability and consequences for all sin. Sin can never be indulged without a cost. And in the context of Adam's sin, God promised the coming of Christ to pay that price by Himself being separated from His Father.

NOTE: The price had to be paid, because GOD CANNOT FORGIVE SIN!!! HE IS HOLY

> *^{44}I am the LORD your God; consecrate yourselves and be holy, because **I am holy**...*
>
> Leviticus 11:44, emphasis added.

God is holy, and cannot countenance sin in any way. Sin demands a price ("*the wages of sin is death*" – Romans 6:23), and when this price is paid, there is nothing to be forgiven! A Holy God demands that the penalty be paid in full, and He Himself has provided for this in His Son, Jesus Christ.

Subsequently, the SINNER **personally** seeks forgiveness, both from God and other sinners. But the sin itself **cannot** be forgiven. Nevertheless, it must be addressed and confessed in order for the sinner to be forgiven.

As a Christian, there is promised forgiveness:

> *^{9}If we confess our sins, **he is faithful and just and will forgive US** our sins and purify us from all unrighteousness.*
>
> 1 John 1:9, emphasis added.

Note that the forgiveness, to us as persons, is premised upon our confession. (See detailed treatment of the issues of confession and forgiveness in Swincer 2016, Chapter 2). This is part of the ongoing life of the Christian, and is different from *initial salvation* and confession for the CAUSATIVE sin noted above. We will return to this point in Chapter 5.

It should be **noted** that there may be a positive operation of the will but sincerely misguided. There are those who are reported in Rome, where:

> ^{8} ... some claim that we say—"Let us do evil that good may result"?
>
> Romans 3:8.

The deliberate choice to sin was purportedly with an honourable purpose! To procure good through evil acts.

In the preceding verse, the Jew even felt that God was indebted to him because his (deliberate) sins highlighted the grace and goodness of God—and God should be grateful to him for his sins!

> ^{7}Someone might argue, "If **my falsehood enhances God's truthfulness and so increases his glory**, why am I still condemned as a sinner?"
>
> Romans 3:8, emphasis added.

Likewise, there were those who wished to gain from God's grace without realising that they were unwittingly debasing it:

> ^{1}What shall we say, then? Shall we go on sinning so that grace may increase? [Holy horrors!!!]
> ^{2}**By no means!** We are those who have died to sin; how can we live in it any longer?
>
> Romans 6:1-2, emphasis added.

Their deliberate choice still resulted in an accountable sin, and no bonus of grace.

2.2.2 The will: NEUTRAL OPERATION

No doubt we have all had the experience of walking across a park in a city, only to find as we are stepping off the lawns to return to the footpath, that we notice a sign in the lawn (and facing the footpath)—not the direction from which we have just come—"DO NOT WALK ON THE GRASS". Too late!! Innocent but guilty!

The will was neutral. There was no deliberate attempt to break some local Council code, but nevertheless the code has been broken. And not withstanding any plea of ignorance, if a ticket is issued, there is a price to be paid.

You may have missed the change of speed limit sign, but that won't deter a zealous law enforcement officer. You are deemed to be guilty.

Sins of ignorance—when the will is in neutral—still attract a penalty.

In the Old Testament, even sins of ignorance (unwitting sins) require atonement. **There is always a cost**.

Leviticus chapter 4 records a section that enumerates the sins of ignorance (or unintentional sins) that apply to the priests (v. 3), the whole community (v. 13), a leader (v. 22), or an individual in the community (v. 27). In each case, atonement had to be made, resulting in the penalty for the sins being paid and the person(s) being forgiven.

**NOTE: It is the sin which is paid—not the person—and the person is forgiven—not the sin!

Even **sins that are undetected**, and that fall in to the category of sins for which atonement must be made, must be accounted for. Deuteronomy addresses the issue of Atonement for an Unsolved Murder:

> *¹If **a man is found slain**, lying in a field in the land the LORD your God is giving you to possess, **and it is not known who killed him**,*
> *²your elders and judges shall go out and measure the distance from the body to the neighbouring towns.*
> *³Then the elders of the town nearest the body shall take a heifer that has never been worked and has never worn a yoke*

⁴*and lead her down to a valley that has not been ploughed or planted and where there is a flowing stream. There in the valley they are to break the heifer's neck.*
⁵*The priests, the sons of Levi, shall step forward, for the LORD your God has chosen them to minister and to pronounce blessings in the name of the LORD and to decide all cases of dispute and assault.*
⁶*Then all the elders of the town nearest the body shall wash their hands over the heifer whose neck was broken in the valley,* ⁷*and they shall declare: "Our hands did not shed this blood, nor did our eyes see it done.*
⁸**Accept this atonement** *for your people Israel, whom you have redeemed, O LORD, and do not hold your people guilty of the blood of an innocent man."* **And the bloodshed will be atoned for.**
⁹*So you will purge from yourselves* **the guilt of shedding innocent blood,** *since you have done what is right in the eyes of the LORD.*

Deuteronomy 21:1-9, emphases added.

Even in the absence of a culprit, sin has been committed and must be addressed by God's people Israel.

Irrespective, ignorance is no grounds for avoiding responsibility. There may be grounds for compassionate consideration, and appeal for leniency, but there can never be blasé indifference.

The removal of sin by the *paying of the price*, thus provides the basis for forgiveness. Forgiveness is not cheap grace:

²⁵*I, even I, am he who blots out your transgressions, for my own sake, and remembers your sins no more.*

Isaiah 43:25.

As noted, even when the sin is **unintentional**, there is still a price to be paid before forgiveness can be given:

> ^{25}*The priest is to **make atonement for the whole Israelite community**, and **they will be forgiven**, for **it was not intentional** and they have brought to the LORD for their wrong an offering made by fire and a sin offering.*
>
> ^{28}*The priest is to make atonement before the LORD for the one who **erred by sinning unintentionally**, and when **atonement** has been made for him, he will **be forgiven**.*
>
> Numbers 15:25, 28, emphases added.

The sinner is forgiven on the basis of the paying of a price (cf. "making restitution", below), **and** as the result of "confession" and "repentance" (below).

2.2.3 The will: NEGATIVE OPERATION— BY-PASSED

**NOTE: PIVOTAL ISSUE #2: THE BY-PASSED WILL, AND ROMANS 7:15-25. (See the Introduction).

Paul faced an intense dilemma in his Christian walk. We need to reflect very carefully on the passage in Romans 7:15-25—**A PIVOTAL PASSAGE.**

A. INTRODUCTION TO ROMANS 7:15-25.

Opinions regarding this passage have been divided three ways (Dunn 1975b, 257). The following three alternatives are a summary of Dunn's observations.

1. Paul's autobiographical account of his own pre-conversion experience.

2. Not autobiographical, but it depicts man in general, or the Jew in particular, apart from Christ, under the law.

3. It describes Paul's own experience even as a believer.

I am bemused by these alternatives, since it seems perfectly obvious that Paul is speaking of his own experience as a Christian (the third alternative). Nothing else seems to make sense from the simple exegesis. However, greater minds than mine have raised these possibilities, so let us briefly examine their merit.

1. Autobiographical – pre-conversion.

This opinion was revived in the early twentieth century by Pietism, in which it is asserted that in Paul's pre-Christian experience he was tormented by his vain attempts to achieve righteousness by his own efforts—as a Pharisee and a persecutor of the early church. The more he tried to keep the law, the more he realised how difficult it was to keep the commandments and to achieve righteousness.

His struggles reach a crescendo as he cries out,

> [18]*I know that nothing good lives in me, that is, in my sinful nature* (sic). *For I have the desire to do what is good, but I cannot carry it out.*
> [19]*For what I do is not the good I want to do; no, the evil I do not want to do—this I keep on doing.*
> [20]*Now if I do what I do not want to do, it is no longer I who do it, but it is sin living in me that does it.*
>
> Romans 7:18-20.

Following from this construct, Romans 8 describes the transition for Paul as he moves from being under the law to being under grace. Supposedly this gives us a better understanding of Paul's attitude to the law, and of his appreciation of the gospel of liberation in his experience. Dunn refers to a book by H. Weinel who cites more than fifty proponents of this interpretation (Dunn 1975b, 257, n.3).

2. Not autobiographical.

"The important monograph by W.G. Kummel in 1929 signalled the end of (the) autobiographical interpretation for most continental scholars" (Dunn 1975b, 258). Romans 7 became Paul's portrayal of man under the law. His use of "I" was a stylistic form to make the story more vivid. This became the basis for Bultmann's existentialist analysis of Paul's theology.

Dunn finds nothing in the chapter that would cause the "I" to be understood in a way that distances Paul from the experience he is describing (1975a, 314). It cannot be reduced to a mere figure of style (314), it is Paul speaking "from the heart of *his own* experience" (314, emphasis his).

3. Autobiographical as a believer.

This is very definitely the minority view in modern exegesis, according to Dunn (1975b, 258). This is the classic view of Augustine and Thomas Aquinas, of Luther and Calvin. In Romans 7 Paul describes his ongoing experience as a believer. Whilst the majority position (#1) saw this as Paul's experience in the past, and about which he now knows nothing—if he ever did—the minority position is that this is a reflection of Paul's present experience even as a Christian.

However, Dunn (1975a) is more comfortable with this position, and with him I concur. He advances two reasons for this.

a. It is the most natural interpretation of Romans 7, both in itself and in its context.

b. It is perfectly consistent with Paul's understanding of grace for the believer in his present walk. And there is nothing that could suggest that the chapter is out of place—it is there by deliberate choice (1975a, 313).

Packer (1964, 622) affirms that since the passage is written totally in the present tense, then grammatically the natural way to read the passage is as a transcript of Paul's self-knowledge and awareness at the time of writing.

The only apparent problem seems to be that the defeated Paul of Chapter 7 is suddenly transformed into the evidently victorious Paul of Chapter 8. But that is more apparent than real.

And note the strong correlation between Romans 7 and 8. The common factors of: the *flesh*, the *Spirit*, and the *habits*. The distress caused by habits in the flesh in Chapter 7, are dealt with by the Spirit helping us to mortify the habits (practices) in Chapter 8:13.

When we correctly understand the position described in Chapter 7 (at least as I see it!), then the wretched man in Chapter 7, as he relates his agonising experience of defeat, acknowledges—already in 7:25—that there is an answer in Christ. That this involves a consenting will through the operation of the Spirit we shall see in Chapter 8:13. And it is clearly a putting to death of the practices of the body: ... *by the Spirit you put to death the misdeeds* [NO "the practices/habits"] *of the body*. Again it becomes clear that a less than adequate translation can cause all manner of misunderstanding. The word is *praxis* (πραξις) from which we can see the transliteration "practices". These were the cause of the problem in Chapter 7, and now the answer is addressed in Chapter 8 (not that the chapter division is of any significance). A failure to address the matter of **practices** has led to all variety of attempts to give an explanation—but they are less than convincing in the perspective of Scripture.

Taking a somewhat different stand, Manson (1959, 162) says that this passage "is a dialectical analysis of the slave-relation so described". He states that the Western Fathers depicted "a transparent account of the Apostle's pre-baptismal experience" (162). This was the position (#1) that Dunn (1975b, 257) noted was revived by Pietism.

By contrast, "the Western Fathers, notably St. Augustine, and the Reformers, especially Calvin ... (have) given the analysis a post-baptismal reference" (Manson 1959, 162). By that he means a reference to his contemporary Christian experience. As noted, Dunn's position.

Personally, I have no difficulty in recognising that Paul is speaking of his own experience as a Christian. This is the plain meaning of the text exegetically, and is more clearly understood when the explanation is given as to the nature of habit sins and how they affect the whole personality, as will be shown in Chapter 4.

B. ADDRESSING THE TEXT (Romans 7:15-25):

> ^{15}I do not understand what I do. For what I want to do I do not do, but what I hate I do.
> ^{16}And if I do what I do not want to do, I agree that the law is good.
> ^{17}As it is, **it is no longer I myself who do it**, but it is sin living in me.
> ^{18}I know that nothing good lives in me, that is, in my sinful nature (sic). For **I have the desire to do what is good, but I cannot carry it out.**
> ^{19}**For what I do is not the good I want to do; no, the evil I do not want to do—this I keep on doing**.
> ^{20}Now if I do what I do not want to do, it is no longer I who do it, but it is sin living in me that does it.
> ^{21}So I find this law at work: When I want to do good, evil is right there with me.
> ^{22}For in my inner being I delight in God's law;
> ^{23}but I see another law at work in the members of my body, waging war against the law of my mind and making me a prisoner of the law of sin at work within my members.
> ^{24}**What a wretched man I am! Who will rescue me from this body of death?**
> ^{25}Thanks be to God—through Jesus Christ our Lord! So then, I myself in my mind am a slave to God's law, but in the sinful nature a slave to the law of sin.
>
> (Emphases added).

Verse 15:

> ^{15}I do not understand what I do. For what I want to do I do not do, but what I hate I do.

We must clarify the word for "do", as it covers a range of meanings, and without this understanding, the text remains very clouded.

- "do". Occurs SIX times in the translation of this verse alone. There are **five** different words for "do" (or a compound).
    - "I **do** not understand": negative of *ginōskō* (γινωσκω). Paul admits that he does not know what is happening. The word—*ginōskō*—simply means "to know—from experience". At this point his experience is somewhat confused, because he does not understand what he is doing.
    - "what I **do**": *katergazomai* (κατεργαζομαι). The root word, *ergazomai*, means "to work"/"do". The prefix, *kata,* indicates an intensive, and thus the whole word means "to work hard"—it is emphatic. It could well mean "work with sweat".
    - "for what **I want to do**": *thelō* (θελω), "to will, to wish". It implies volition and purpose, and frequently a determination (Vine, *et al*, 1996, Vol. 2, 162). In the confusion, Paul has a determination, but he is not delivering!
    - "I **do** not do": *prassō* (πρασσω): meaning "to do, to practice". Paul's **practice**, is not the result of his own determination. In fact, he actually does things of which he does not approve—although he once did! However, he is unwittingly actually **practicing** things **learned** in the past and which are now automatic, by-passing his will—to his extreme consternation. **Note, practice is learned behaviour.**

- "but what I hate I **do**": *poieō* (ποιεω): "to do, make," is used of spending a time or tarrying, in a place (Vine, *et al*, 1996, Vol. 2, 2).

NOTE: the six verbs (with five different words) in verse 15 (alone) are all first person and in the present tense, indicating that this is **Paul's ongoing experience.

PARAPHRASE:

Let us attempt a paraphrase to try to understand these several words for "do":

*What I am working so hard at (**do**ing), I **do** not understand (know), but what I will (strongly desire) to **do** is bypassed, and I **do** not **practice** that. On the contrary, what I hate, I end up **do**ing* [which is in fact what he had previously practiced!].

Paul's present behaviour—practice—is not instigated by his will. Hence they are not volitional acts at that time. In spite of Paul's determination, he is acting contrary to his will. **His will is bypassed.** However, this is no excuse to assert that there is a "sinful nature" or some third party that is operating in Paul's body without his consent. That is precisely the basis of much of the misunderstanding of this passage.

For ex ample, Barth states:

> It is not I who am at work, but—unfortunately **I am not master of my own house**—the sin which dwelleth in me … I have to admit to myself that I am only a kind of agent and not the subject, that I am only a functioning object …
>
> Barth 1956, 588, emphasis added.

Wrong. I **am** master of my own house and I have choices to make, and I need to do it responsibly. And Paul has made these choices voluntarily and deliberately in the past until they became learned behaviours, that is, practices/habits.

Now he just does them without thinking—and in fact when he does think about them he finds that his reflexes are just too fast and he sins before he realises. This behaviour needs to be addressed.

- "will": *thelō* (θελω), as noted, this implies volition and purpose, and often a strong sense of determination. It is in the present infinitive, and as such denotes "being constantly desirous". So it is not a lack of determination that is Paul's problem. This is emphasised by his contrary action as follows: *what I hate I do*. He doesn't realise how strong and natural his habits have become.

- "hate": *misō* (μισω): "to hate," is used especially of malicious and unjustifiable feelings towards others, whether towards the innocent or by mutual animosity, but also an aversion from what is evil (Vine, *et al*, 1996, Vol. 2, 292)). It is a strong expression. The very things that Paul despises, are in fact the things that he ends up doing.

Verse 16:

[16] And if I do what I do not want to do, I agree that the law is good.

- "I agree that the law is good" (see also verse 12). Although Paul breaks the law, he doesn't want to, and he is acknowledging that it is good, because his conscience testifies that it is wrong to break it.

Verse 17:

[17] As it is it is no longer I myself who do it, but it is sin living in me

This is the defensive cry of Paul as he notes the two facts from verse 15: (1) he is not doing what he wants, (2) but he is doing what he doesn't want.

- "sin living in me". Having exonerated the law—it is good—Paul concludes that since he is no longer performing voluntarily, the reason is due to ingrained sin. But this is not a "nature". There is an inculcated pattern of response through his body that bypasses his brain and his will. It is a reflex action, and because it is wrong it is described as sin.

Verse 18:

¹⁸I know that nothing good lives in me, that is, in my sinful nature (sic). *For I have the desire to do what is good, but I cannot carry it out.*

Paul confirms this dilemma with which he is grappling.

- "in my sinful nature": *en tē sarki mou* (ἐν τη σαρκι μου). Literally "in my flesh". IT IS NOT "MY SINFUL NATURE". Flesh is not a sinful nature. This translation aberration is the source of serious misunderstanding. Paul uses the word "flesh" because he means—under the inspiration of the Holy Spirit—to use the word flesh!! Let me quote from Dr Ted Gibson:

  > A growing child receives stimuli. These operate on three levels—body, emotions, and mind. The stimuli are at the very beginning almost totally physical, but other aspects gradually increase. To every stimulus comes the reaction of the ego and a development of drives to satisfy the stimuli. There develop **habits** of reaction in purely physical things, in emotional matters, in mental states. These have been produced by the reaction of a sinful self-centred ego. Thus the patterns of reaction created in the body are the **patterns or practices** of the Old Man – from putting on a jumper [sweater] to reacting to a punch on the nose; from saying "thank you" when given something to swearing when insulted. Of course some **habits**, like putting on a jumper, are quite physically neutral—neither good nor bad. But the mass of our reactions is impregnated by the self of the Old Man. When a person becomes a Christian his ego is changed. The Holy Spirit regenerates

and lives in and with the regenerated ego. But the paths of the patterns created in the body by the Old Man remain and have to be replaced by new paths and new patterns (as required) [**new habits**] to conform with the required reactions of the New Man. The introduction of the New Man is associated immediately with pattern changing—much of the old life immediately disappears in the upsurge of new life. There is always an area of living or aspects of living in which new patterns need to be deliberately created [**new learned habit reactions**]. Growth in grace is associated with increasing awareness of what the Spirit desires to alter, and increasing the fixity of faith's patterns in our behaviour.

Gibson n.d., 3, emphases added.

Gibson is seeking to explain the dilemma that is apparently in these verses. The "flesh" is precisely what Paul means as he explains that inculcated within his flesh (meat/grey matter) are learned reactions or habits. Habits bypass the will. They are no longer matters of the mind and will. See the next section for treatment of the term "the flesh".

As Gibson has noted, many habits are quite innocuous. I always use the Windsor Knot for tying my tie—as long as I don't get tied up in knots! After repeated tyings, it has become quite natural—in fact a habit. Now if I stop and try to think it through I just mess up the whole process. It is easier to "just do it". It is similar with tying up shoe laces, and there are many examples of these neutral habits. There are also many examples of negative habits, of ways of thinking in a variety of circumstances that are not helpful or God-honouring. These are in the problem area.

NOTE: These actions did not bypass the will **originally. They were behaviours that were **consented** to repeatedly until they became automatic. In the non-Christian condition, there were behaviours that resulted from the sinful condition. As noted, sinners sin because they are sinners. It is "normal" but not compulsory to sin. It is in this state—the Old Man condition—that these behaviours were learned and exercised.

When a person is converted, he accepts the death of the Old Man, and accepts the New Man, with a range of new behaviours. But there are residual habits "in the flesh" that have to now be "put to death". The Christian did not lose his actual flesh in which are inculcated the habits.

We will take this matter up shortly, but in the meantime, to return to the context of Romans 7:18.

Paul is at a loss. He just cannot do what he wants, and he is increasingly exasperated.

- "the desire": *thelō* (θελω)—the will—as in verse 15.

- "(I cannot) carry it out": *katergazomai* (κατεργαζομαι)— again the same as verse 15.

- "I cannot": *ouch heuriskō* (οὐχ εὑρσικω): literally, "I am not able to find". Paul cannot find out why he cannot carry out his desires, but instead does the very opposite. See further on verse 20.

Verse 19:

[19]For what I do (poieō) is not the good I want (thelō—wish) to do; no, the evil I do not want to do (thelō—wish)—this I keep on doing (prassō—practising).

Note the recurrence of the same words as in verse 15. And in particular, note that Paul is not **practicing** what he has the strong desire to do. Again, he laments the fact that **his will is bypassed.** His practice is evil. And there seems to be nothing that he can do about it.

Some have interpreted this to mean that Paul is compelled by "his old sin nature", or "his sinful nature", verse 18. But that is an incorrect translation as we have noted, and shall note in more detail shortly.

In the meantime, Paul's dilemma is intensified as he states in:

Verse 20:

> [20] Now if I do what I do not want to do, it is no longer I who do it, but it is sin living in me that does it.

The explanation seems to be that his will is being bypassed by *"sin living in me that does it"*. These are the learned sinful responses of man as a psychosomatic unity. Sin is not an entity, but his body and mind have worked in conjunction, so that responses **by consent** (a consenting will), have now become inculcated in his body—his flesh—so that they are now automatic—habits.

Up to now, if someone treads on Paul's toe, he does not stop to think what the suitable response might be, past experience has dictated that you punch the guy in the mouth and ask questions later. It is automatic. But now as a Christian, he has to rethink his whole approach. He doesn't want to punch anybody, but his reflexes take over if his toe is trodden on. Someone treads on his toe. Whack! And as the person is picking himself up off the floor Paul is apologising profusely. "I'm sorry. I didn't mean to. O wretched man that I am. Who will deliver me from this body of death?"

The event is all too quick and automatic, and it by-passes his mind and his will. And so he laments (using a rather free paraphrase of Romans 7:15-20):

> [15] I do not understand what I am doing. For what I want to do—not punch the other bloke—I end up doing. So I am doing what I hate to do [punch the other bloke]), *now that I am a Christian.* [16] And if I do what I do not want to do—punch the other bloke, I agree that the law is good. So there is not a problem with the law—it is good [verse 12: So then, the law is holy, and the commandment is holy, righteous and good.]

¹⁷As it is, it is no longer I myself who do it—because my will is being bypassed—but it is sin living in me. A habit response learned as a non-Christian (or even as a Christian).
¹⁸I know that nothing good lives in me, that is, in my flesh [NOT "in my sinful nature"—the word is sarx – σαρξ]. *For I have the desire to do what is good, but I cannot carry it out. Patterned in my flesh* [including the grey matter!] *are the learned reactions of the Old Man—the unregenerate way of life.*
¹⁹For what I am actually doing is not the good I strongly desire to do; no, the evil that I equally strongly desire not to do—this I keep on practicing—that is, a learned response by repetition.
²⁰Now if I do what I do not want to do, it is no longer I who do it, but it is sin living in me that does it. Not that my hand is forced, but that there are habit responses that just take over as reflex actions.

Paul is faced with a whole new learning experience—how to replace the old habits, and how to learn new "habits" or appropriate reactions to the same circumstances.

Verses 21:

²¹So I find this law at work: When I want to do good, evil is right there with me.

- Paul finds a new law as it were, or a principle: *When I want to do good, evil is right there with me.* Paul is at a loss to explain his actions. But he does recognise that there is somehow an alternative law at work when he is seeking to enact his desires. But we must not jump to the worn out conclusion that this is some "sin-nature" or "flesh" with an independent personality and determinative powers. See above on verse 18.

Verse 22:

²²For in my inner being I delight in God's law;

Paul again is at pains to affirm his acceptance of the goodness of God's law—cf. verse 12: *So then, the law is **holy**, and the commandment is **holy**, righteous and **good*** (emphases added), and verse 16: ... *I agree that the law is good.*

Verse 23:

²³but I see another law at work in the members of my body, waging war against the law of my mind and making me a prisoner of the law of sin at work within my members.

- Paul identifies this new law (from verse 21) as *the law of sin.* But this is not the flesh. It is the habit responses located in the flesh. See above on verse 18.

Verse 24:

²⁴What a wretched man I am! Who will rescue me from this body of death?

- For a man of such learning, wisdom and discipline, it is embarrassing to have to admit such abject failure. He feels wretched and defeated. What possibility is there of deliverance? Only through Jesus Christ.

- "body of death". Most commentators lapse straight into an explanation based on the idea of the "old sinful nature" or equivalent. There is no need to do this. Paul is struggling with the fact that inculcated within his flesh (his body) are patterned responses which are condemning him—and in effect producing death. He wants deliverance from this seemingly impossible situation. And most people can identify with this feeling of desperation, frustration and exhaustion. But there is an answer.

Verse 25:

²⁵Thanks be to God—through Jesus Christ our Lord! So then, I myself in my mind am a slave to God's law, but in the sinful nature (sic) *a slave to the law of sin.*

- "Thanks be to God—through Jesus Christ our Lord!" There is hope. He can be rescued from "this body of death"—but it is not just a clichéd answer. Paul feels that he is attempting to serve two masters:

1. In his mind he is committed to the good law:

    *²⁵ ... So then, I myself **in my mind** am a slave to God's law, ...*

Paul has clearly acknowledged that God's law is good and holy, and that he wants to earnestly obey it,

2. But in his flesh he is performing out of habit:

    *²⁵ ... but **in the** ~~sinful nature~~ [**flesh**] a slave to the law of sin.*

His mind is committed to God's law, but his body is not in sync. It is operating without reference to his mind.

Whichever way, Paul has only himself to blame. **He is responsible for his sin:**

1. Initially **he is responsible** for his sin to become a sinner, and hence the Old Man condition in which he learned to sin repeatedly, resulting in habits.

2. Under the mastery of either Christ or Satan by his own volition (cf. Romans 6:16, see below) as a Christian, he still acts by choice, and if he sins it is deliberate sin and **he is responsible**.

3. But there is also behaviour by reflex action—good or bad—APART FROM VOLITION in the immediate context, but initially learned by repeated volition. This is Paul's dilemma. Because he consented to the behaviours which are now habits, **he is responsible**.

CONCLUSION re ROMANS 7:15-25.

The only satisfactory way to understand Romans 7:15-25, is by recognising the operation of habit behaviours. Man always has to be responsible for his actions, and delegating his actions to a third party is foreign to Scripture. This resolution will be shown more clearly when we look at the responses to the three categories of sin in Chapter 4, as well as the treatment of Paul's victory achieved through the teaching of Romans 8 as we shall see in Chapter 5.

C. SUMMARY CONCERNING THE WILL.

1. Our wills are never abrogated.
2. Our wills are never negated by "bias" or "tendencies".
3. Our wills are never forced by a third party "nature" or "flesh".
4. Our wills are involved in all sin—the three categories noted below.

2.3 THE FLESH (NOT "NATURE")

**NOTE: PIVOTAL ISSUE #3: THE FLESH. (See the Introduction).

The mistranslation of this word is so significant that it is essential that we clarify its usage and meaning. Together with the mistranslation of the Old Man/New Man, they are a large part of the cause of the whole problem regarding the Christian and responsibility for personal sin.

The fallacy of interpreting "flesh" as "sinful nature" with some type of determinative power, has already been noted in the treatment of Romans 7:15-25. We now look at it more directly, as a pivotal issue in the whole debate.

The Greek word for "flesh" is *sarx* (σαρξ):

1 flesh (the soft substance of the living body, which covers the bones and is permeated with blood) of both man and beasts. **2** the body. **2A** the body of a man. **2B** used of natural or physical origin, generation or relationship. *2B1* born of natural generation. **2C** the sensuous nature of man, "the animal nature".

2c1 without any suggestion of depravity. *2c2* the animal nature with cravings which incite to sin. *2c3* the physical nature of man as subject to suffering. **3** a living creature (because possessed of a body of flesh) whether man or beast. **4** the flesh, denotes mere human nature, the earthly nature of man apart from divine influence, and therefore prone to sin and opposed to God. [Strong 1996].

Strong very accurately portrays the meanings, except at 2c2 (and 4), as distinct from 2c1, where the flesh has a personalized aspect "with cravings which incite to sin". He notes that there are 151 occurrences of *sarx*; and the AV translates as "flesh" 147 times, "carnal" twice, "carnally minded + 5427" once, and "fleshly" once. If other translators kept to this accuracy there would be very little problem. But the majority of translators interpret, rather than translate, and render the word as "sinful nature", and give to the flesh a personality and a will as a separate part of the person. This is extremely misleading, and has been refuted as we looked at the matter of the will on the one hand, and now also as we look at the operation of the flesh on the other.

However, on the other end of the spectrum, is the fact that the same "translators" render Old Man as the "sinful nature", or the "old nature", thus confusing two quite separate entities. This will also be refuted in Chapter 3, THE OLD MAN.

By way of perspective, the Greek word for nature, *phusis* (φυσις), occurs only 14 times in the New Testament, and it is used to indicate the nature of a person or things or events, but it never addresses anything like "the flesh". Hence to translate "flesh" as nature is quite misleading. Certainly to imply that a nature (or the flesh) has determinative powers or is a moral agent is quite fallacious.

Often the flesh is portrayed as inseparable from evil, and that humanity is **incurably** evil. Does that imply that salvation is impossible? The flesh is given personality and a will that is supposedly far stronger than our own. (Where does this personalised "flesh" live?) Or we are supposed to have "an inward propensity, an inner tendency toward evil which is present and felt even when the will is set against it" (Taylor 1945, 102). Supposedly we have a bias against which we have no power. There are two wills within us!!??

Often it is suggested that the cure to the problem is "subdue the flesh by walking in the Spirit". That is a simplistic idea to the concept of the "flesh", again having some entity of its own, that it can be subjugated.

I do not find this portrayal in Scripture.

2.3.1 INTRODUCTION

Briefly looking at a few examples in the literature, where **flesh** is addressed/defined, we immediately see the fundamental theological problem.

Ridgway (1978) is typical of the efforts that are made at trying to infuse some understanding into the "flesh", and in particular to try to give it some sense of entity with powers of determination. He gives a laboured differentiation of flesh, starting with two broad categories: ethical and non-ethical. He traces steps in the intensification of the ethical meaning (2). He then looks at the portrayal of flesh as a "liability" (!!) in Romans 6 and 8, and also Galatians 3 and 5 (3-12). He attempts to differentiate many shades of meaning for the term, but mostly he seeks to show that the flesh has an independent identity that robs a person of the ability to make decisions: "consequently there is spiritual **impotence to do good and to resist evil**", "**incapable** of meeting the demands of the Divine Law". He says that the flesh describes "human nature (sic) infected by sin", of taking on "the character of **opposition or rivalry**", of being "infected, influenced and **controlled** by sin", of being "spiritually **impotent** and ineffectual", as "an ethically evil force", that it is "personified as a corrupting force in man in that **it has lusts**", "as active and **the source of sinful acts**" (5-7, emphases added).

I am amazed at these conclusions. I am not aware of a second or third party in my life forcing my hand quite independently and making it impossible for me to make my own decisions. This is the basic problem of why Christians are looking for an escape from personal responsibility and accountability. The truth is that we each have a will, and we make choices—but not always the right ones!

Likewise, **Criswell** (1973, 137) confuses the terms. He takes the Old Man, and calls that the "old nature" (also "the depraved human nature" [138]) but then identifies that with the flesh, specifically acknowledging the Greek for flesh as *sarx*. In turn the flesh becomes "personalised" as producing "our fleshly passions". But the flesh does not have independent determination in our bodies—we do not have other attached appendages that are controlling us without consultation!!

Criswell states that as long as we are "in the body" we shall be accompanied by "trials and temptations that come from the *black drops of sin in our blood*" (137, emphasis added). That might well make a dramatic preaching point, but it certainly has no credence or biblical foundation. Unfortunately, too often it is statements by revered Bible teachers that become common parlance for perceived biblical realities that set the tone for error in theological understanding and belief. Later we shall notice a similar impact of the concepts expressed by Dr Martyn Lloyd-Jones and Major Ian Thomas. The fact that these cases are dated does not change the principle.

Criswell suggests that there is a constant warfare between "our two natures" (137). We don't have any natures in the sense being suggested. The Bible speaks very clearly about *the flesh* and *the Spirit*. But the flesh is no more a dominating party than is the Spirit. You can't have it both ways. If we are controlled by the flesh then we are equally controlled by the Spirit. So we just sit back in the grandstand and watch the fight!?

And any "control" by the Spirit is a consequence of our consenting will—as we will note in Chapter 5—and not independently of it.

No. We are the location in which WE (not the "sinful nature" as some part of us) have normal desires and appetites. We can act with the will—no one is forcing our hands—to pursue those appetites to a reasonable conclusion (eat a normal meal) or we can choose to take it to an extreme (gluttony) where it becomes a problem. If we keep in tune with the Spirit, we will be helped to act responsibly and be acutely aware when things are getting out of hand.

Hoekema (1987, 84), in spite of his other correctives concerning the Old Man (as distinct from nature—see later), personifies the flesh, at least in regard to Galatians 5:16-17: "Though the word *flesh* (emphasis his) as used in the New Testament may have various meanings, here it means the tendency within human beings to disobey God in every area of life". There is no such inherent bias in the flesh. We are sinners, and sinners sin! It is not a "tendency", it is a choice.

Strong ignores the word "flesh" and simply uses the word "nature", and he identifies it directly with sin and gives it determinative powers.

> Every member of the human race, without exception, possesses a corrupted nature, which is **a source of actual sin, and is itself sin.**
>
> Strong 1907, 577, emphasis added.

What amazing nonsense. What is this "nature" that is a "source of actual sin"? Where is this third party producing sin in the human being? Even more bizarre is the assertion that this "nature" "**is itself sin**". How? Sin is not a commodity, and unless this "nature" has some independent operation and a will to exercise and therefore choose to sin, the whole idea is preposterous. And how does this relate to the "host" human being? Is he guilty because this third party went ape? No wonder there is such strange thinking in the Christian population.

And Strong is not being misrepresented here, because he states emphatically (1907, 577-8, emphases added):

> The sinful acts and dispositions of men are referred to, **and explained by, a corrupt nature** ... By 'nature' we mean that which is *born* (emphasis his) in a man, that which he has by birth. That there is **an inborn corrupt state**, from which sinful acts and dispositions flow ... This corrupt nature (a) belongs to man from the first moment of his being; (b) underlies man's consciousness; (c) **cannot be changed by man's own power**; (d) first constitutes him a sinner before God ...

Well that lets us off the hook! I cannot change the situation! I have a corrupt nature, so don't blame me. And when I can locate this corrupt nature I'll give him a hiding. What nonsense.

When I choose to sin, I will sin, and I will wear the responsibility and the guilt. And I will confess my culpability and I will receive the forgiveness offered in Christ (1 John 1:9). **There is no third party**.

I have never encountered this corrupt nature that "**cannot be changed by man's own power**". I have never had a discussion with this third party before sinning—but of course according to Strong, the "corrupt nature" would have already acted quite independently of me, and beyond my power to say otherwise anyhow! Rubbish.

And Strong states that "this sin" (meaning this "corrupt nature") goes back to the moment of conception (578). So what is sin? The act of procreation? We have already noted Strong's erroneous concept of sin in the definition at #A. Sin is not inherited. It is not a commodity to be traded or handed down. Sin is the act of the will in opposition to God as we noted earlier.

Contrary to this, Strong would say, "men are evil, because they are born evil" (578). This view has been refuted in the former volume, *Condemned Already* (Swincer, 2011a). That is, "condemnation by generation".

Perhaps the worst of Strong's errors is found in his assertion that the will is made a moral agent that is already corrupted: "Sin is a nature, in the sense of a **congenital depravity of the will** ... This nature is **guilty and condemnable**" (578, emphases added). This is also "condemnation by generation". According to Strong, we are *Condemned Already* through no fault of our own, but simply because we were born. Μη γενοιτο! Holy horrors!

Nowhere does the Bible say that "All have a 'corrupted nature' and come short of the glory of God" (Romans 3:23). Nowhere does the Bible say that "The wages of having a 'corrupted nature' is death" (Romans 6:23). The Bible does not say, "And so death passed to all men because all men have 'corrupted natures'" (Romans 5:12).

It is amazing that for over 100 years the influence of Strong (assisted by others) has affected theological thinking, until like the ingrained habits of the Old Man, the Christian world has an ingrained response to these unbiblical views concerning man and his responsibility. The influence concerning the "sin-nature" or "corrupt nature" that does not exist, has been given cogency and unquestioning acceptance by the Christian public with barely a whimper of objection or discernment about the truth of God's Word. Most people seem to happily parrot the same old clichés with no awareness of Biblical parameters. Where are the theologians?

However, there is a part corrective found in **Brunner** when he says, "Sin is never a state [or position, or nature, etc.], but it is **always an act**" (cited in Berkhof 1939, 249, emphasis added). Rightly **Berkhof** draws attention to the fact that "in Brunner's estimation the traditional view has an **undesirable element of determinism in it, and does not sufficiently safeguard the responsibility of man**" (249, emphasis added). Bravo!

Bultmann has a more balanced view initially. He states clearly the perspective that the flesh is **man's body**—not just as "meat"—but as **animate flesh**. It is the body with its sensual manifestations (1952, 233), "though it does primarily mean a material, it means a material only as it is formed and animated in the human body" (233).

Further, it can be used to **designate the person himself**:

*⁵For, when we were come into Macedonia, **our flesh had no rest**, but we were troubled on every side;*

2 Corinthians 7:5, AV, emphasis added.

In this context Bultmann does not suggest that the flesh (as the body/self) has an independent existence or is self-determining. It is precisely a means of speaking of the person (Paul and his companions, in this case) but indicating the weakness of the flesh (body) under the troubles experienced. They were simply exhausted!

Additionally, the flesh may signify characteristics of our **humanness**, in its "weakness and transitoriness" (234).

There is also a "**physiological**" connotation. One can "glory after the flesh", or "boast of worldly things" (2 Corinthians 11:18) (235).

Then there is the indication of the **sphere in which one moves**: "the sphere which marks out the horizon or the possibilities of what he does and experiences" (235). Hence, "to lead one's life as a man", where there are no ethical or moral judgments, but just taking note of the fact (236).

Flesh may also indicate a "**natural progenitor**", as is the case when referring to Abraham (237):

> *¹What then shall we say that **Abraham** our father has found **according to the flesh**? ...*
>
> Romans 4:1, emphases added.

Further, Bultmann says that the term "flesh" can also be used to "**modify substantives**" (237). Instead of flesh simply indicating life/existence as "natural-human", there is an attitude, of walking, knowing, acting, warring—after the flesh (237). These are in fact attitudes where the normal fleshly desires are pursued as an end in themselves.

Having done an excellent job in defining the concept and understanding of the flesh in its variety of usages, Bultmann then goes on to look at the flesh and sin. He raises two options:

1. whether a man's life "in the flesh" is a stage, in the sense noted above, or
2. whether it is the "**determinative norm**" (239, emphasis added).

He seems to be opening the door for the usual idea of "personification" of the flesh, and of it having "determinative" abilities. Looking at Galatians 5:13:

> *¹³For you, brethren, have been called to liberty; only do not use liberty as **an opportunity for the flesh** ...*
>
> Galatians 5:13, (NKJV) emphasis added,

he points out that this is just "natural human self-seeking" (239). But just when it seems that he has kept the biblical position, he says, the "fact that '*flesh*', and through it also '*sin*', *can become powers* to which man falls slave ..." (244, emphases his), he has given "the flesh" an independent power to determine and operate. And in case we are guessing, he continues, "this language stamps *flesh and sin as powers to which man has fallen victim* and against which he is **powerless**" (245, italics his, bold added). So now we have a separate and independent power—against which we are powerless—and to which we have become the victims.

So we are no longer responsible for our sins. We are powerless to resist.

Although **Bultmann** seemed to have the basic concept of the "flesh" well defined, he lapsed into the common position of making the flesh personal, that is, with personality and determination.

And not surprisingly he then looks at Romans 7. We shall come back to this pivotal passage shortly.

But we must ask before moving on: Where does this independent power reside? And how does he/it operate? What biblical basis is there for such a concept? I have found no answers to this enquiry.

Brunner (1952, 109), whilst not personalizing "nature", muddies the waters by not specifically stating man's responsibility, but that "we can say that sins arise out of our sinful state as the fruit is produced by the tree". There seems to be something automatic here rather than something determined by the person. Nevertheless, he does clarify that "Sins do not grow as a natural necessity ... as crab apples grow on a crab apple tree". At least he recognizes that although there is something "automatic" like the production of fruit, nevertheless it is not imperative. He says, "It is true ... that once a man has become a sinner all that he does is infected by sin ... But a particular sin does not of necessity follow from the state of sin. The fact that 'I am sinner' does not mean that I **must** tell lies, steal, commit adultery, or murder." (109, emphasis added). He thus affirms that man has a will to act independently, and is therefore not under compulsion to a "nature", or even his "sinful state".

Morris (1960, 82) starts with a very balanced point of view, acknowledging that the flesh is simply the outward visible part of us, that can also be used to refer to life in the body (flesh), and because of imperfection the term can be used to refer to our imperfections. He then succumbs to the common error of referring to the flesh as "the fleshly nature" (84), or as "the lower nature" (86), and implies the idea of an entity that is capable of being opposed to the Spirit. Further, in stating that "The Spirit's work in overcoming our lower nature (sic) …" he gives this lower nature a personality that is able to be overcome (subjugated).

There is no biblical basis for this idea of personalising the flesh. The basic drives and desires of the flesh are normal, natural and healthy—but they don't have a will.

Taylor (1945, 102) implies that the flesh has an independence in our lives, and is "Constantly clamouring for the consent of the will, and when that consent is given, an act of sin is committed …". But Paul gives a different picture:

> [13]***Do not offer the parts of your body to sin***, *as instruments of wickedness, but rather **offer yourselves to God**, as those who have been brought from death to life; and **offer** the parts of your body **to him** as instruments of righteousness.*
>
> Romans 6:13, emphases added.

Paul sees us as being in control, and **we** make the choice to whom we will offer ourselves. Taylor believes that we have "inbred sin as a tendency or state" (1945, 103), a bias as well as a "clamouring" power. What is the nature and residence of this supposed independent power that is able to contest with our wills? It certainly is not found in biblical evidence.

Smith (1983) is one of the few writers who seems to have a balanced biblical view of the flesh. He expresses his concern that "nature"—the term used for flesh so frequently—is never carefully discussed, and more astonishingly he finds that the "two-nature" concept is never challenged (1983, 19).

He reflects my concern, that the word "nature" has been treated as though it designates a substance without clarification or distinction (18). He asks, "is there another metaphysical entity (or even two additional entities [including the soul]) inside a man which should be labelled as a 'nature' (or as two natures)?" (19).

Additionally, he refers to the orthodox creeds, where both Chalcedon and Westminster "refer to the 'properties' of a nature as though it were a substance" (19), which he further clarifies as we shall see. But he also notes that Hodge—the author of a most notable theology text—in defining nature, recognises that although only an objective entity can act, nevertheless the "idea of substance is a necessary one" in order to understand nature (cited in Smith 1983, 19). But this is only possible if one had already concluded that a "nature" can and does act, and in the case of humans, that means being morally responsible.

But Smith points out, "**the Bible never speaks of a nature as acting**" (19, emphasis his). Smith finds that Hodge contradicts himself as he discusses the regeneration of man, where his definition of substance is changed, as he states that the "new nature" (sic) is not a substance added alongside the "old nature" (sic) (19).

> Reformed theologians have, in general, followed the pattern of Hodge both in his wrong definition of nature as substance and in his fortuitous inconsistency in teaching that the new nature is not a substance added alongside the old nature.
>
> Smith 1983, 19.

Smith finds that as distinct from the Reformed theologians, Dispensationalists usually apply substance to both the new nature (sic) as well as the old nature (sic).

He concludes, "the Bible never uses the term 'nature' (Greek *phusis*) in the sense that theologians have spoken of an 'old nature'" (19). He notes that the term "nature" does not designate a substance or an entity, "Instead it is a word which refers to the inherent or essential qualities of any substance or entity" (20). A "nature" is not a person and therefore has no moral responsibility, nor ability to act morally or otherwise.

Buswell (cited in Smith 1983, 20) seeks to clarify:

> A person is a non-material substantive entity, and is not to be confused with a nature. A nature is not a *part* of person in the substantive sense. A nature is a complex of attributes, and is not to be confused with a substantive entity.
>
> (Emphasis Buswell's).

Only persons can sin, and only persons can be morally responsible. The whole concept of a nature compelling or forcing the hand of a person to sin is foreign to Scripture, and is most misleading.

2.3.2 EXAMPLES OF THE FLESH—OBJECTIVELY

As we have noted, there is no biblical basis for this idea of personalising the flesh. The basic drives and desires of the flesh are normal, natural and healthy. Consider this basic drive:

- There is nothing wrong with **food**, *per se*. As noted above, if eating becomes out of control or if our wills have yielded so often that it becomes a habit, then the result could well become sin.

After a particularly tiring hike on a bitterly cold day, returning to the warmth of the home one might feel ravenous, "I could eat a horse!" This natural desire has reached new heights, and one might be prepared to go to extremes to satisfy this natural hunger—but there is no third party "calling the shots". You don't in fact **have** to eat, whatever the sense of compulsion.

If smoke starts pouring from the kitchen this would introduce new information to the mind, leading to that information being processed in such a way that the hunger suddenly becomes very insignificant in the face of a new need—survival in the face of fire. The will is activated by the mind, and results in a personal decision—no one else is involved as if a nature embedded in the body was controlling the person. YOU decide to flee, or try to douse the fire, or call the fire brigade, or all of the above. But **you** make the choice. And it might be a further three hours before that ravenous hunger is finally satiated, even if at the time you thought that you only had minutes to live!

Esau had been out hunting one day, and on returning home he found his brother working in the kitchen and producing an assault on the olfactories even under normal circumstances, let alone on this occasion when he was particularly vulnerable:

> *²⁹Once when Jacob was cooking some stew, Esau came in from the open country, famished.*
> *³⁰He said to Jacob, "Quick, let me have some of that red stew! **I'm famished**!" ...*
> *³¹Jacob replied, "First sell me your birthright."*
> *³²"Look, **I am about to die**," Esau said. "What good is the birthright to me?"*
> *³³But Jacob said, "Swear to me first." So he swore an oath to him, selling his birthright to Jacob.*
> *³⁴Then Jacob gave Esau some bread and some lentil stew. He ate and drank, and then got up and left. So **Esau despised his birthright**.*

Genesis 25:29-34, emphases added.

Esau was under the control of no third party. **He was held responsible**—*Esau despised his birthright*. Sure he felt "famished", and even thought he was about to die, but he had a choice. And his choice was to "despise his birthright" which was a very significant issue in his culture. It involved a double portion of the father's inheritance (Deuteronomy 21:17), and also included "chieftainship", the rule over his brothers and the entire family (Genesis 27:29), and the title to the blessing of the promise (Genesis 27:4, 27-29) (Keil and Delitzsch 1980, 268-9).

Later, when his appetite had been satisfied, and he had time to reflect on the situation, Esau wanted to recover what he had been responsible for "signing away" by his own decision, but it was too late. The operation of his will to reverse the situation was ineffective, and he was totally responsible. His capriciousness serves as a warning to all (Hebrews 12:16-17):

> ^{16}*See that no one ... is godless like Esau, who for a single meal sold his inheritance rights as the oldest son.*
> ^{17}*Afterward, as you know, when he wanted to inherit this blessing, he was rejected. He could bring about no change of mind, though he sought the blessing with tears.*

Another basic drive:

- There is nothing wrong with **sex**, *per se*. God created it. He said:

  > ^{27}*So God created man in his own image ...*
  > ^{28}*God blessed them and said to them, "**Be fruitful and increase in number;** fill the earth ...*

  Genesis 1:27-28, emphasis added.

But if sex becomes all-consuming so that we indulge in fornication and immorality *inter alia*, then we will have included the things that Jesus condemned—and it doesn't have to be the overt act only:

> ^{27}*"You have heard that it was said, 'Do not commit adultery.'*
> ^{28}*But I tell you that anyone who **looks at a woman lustfully has already committed adultery** with her in his heart.*

Matthew 5:27-28, emphasis added.

Sex is a normal part of married life. And any initiation of the continuum leading to consummation is to be expected. But there is no third party forcing the hand of either of the married couple. It is an act of the will—a choice. However, if both are not consenting, then a difficulty arises. But there is still no third party driving the relationship. It is—and always remains—a choice.

There is no compulsion, but if one party becomes demanding or manipulative then love is no longer the motivating factor and the whole situation becomes selfish and therefore sinful. And that is within the normal marriage relationship. It can have more serious consequences if the desire is outside of marriage and deteriorates to lust and then adultery or some such.

Equally, the desire to pursue the natural desires leading to consummation will progress through stages of mounting tension, but none of these is intrinsically wrong nor is it driven by the flesh as if it were a third party. And to demonstrate that the will is still fundamentally involved, should the procedure be interrupted, **the mind—the most important sex organ**—will make a decision leading to a determination of the will, but **it is not the flesh**—as some independent driving force.

The smell of smoke and the shrill blare of an alarm will lead the mind to make a determination—and inevitably there will be a sudden change of plans in the bedroom! But there is no "fleshly compulsion" that changes the parameters.

Or let the evening be interrupted by a blood-curdling scream just outside the bedroom window, and it will be the mind that makes a determination that something is wrong and consummation may suddenly be relegated to second place irrespective of how intense the desire.

- There is nothing wrong with **money**, *per se*. But if we set our hearts on it, it becomes the cause of evil and can have disastrous results (1 Timothy 6:10, emphasis added):

*[10]For the **love** of money is a root of all kinds of evil. Some people, eager for money, have wandered from the faith and pierced themselves with many griefs.*

Lest the shepherds of God's flock become corrupted by bribes or influenced by good salary packages, Peter exhorts:

*²Be shepherds of God's flock that is under your care, serving as overseers—not because you must, but because you are willing, as God wants you to be; **not greedy for money**, but eager to serve;*

1 Peter 5:2, emphasis added.

The Psalmist gives a general warning concerning riches:

¹⁰Do not trust in extortion or take pride in stolen goods; though your riches increase, do not set your heart on them.

Psalm 62:10.

Money is a basic commodity in society, and essential in some form or other, but given the wrong motivation, all types of evil in corruption, bribes, extortion, stealing, etc. may result—all as the outcome of the direct operation of our wills. And we will be held responsible. No one goes to court and pleads his case on the basis that his "old nature" made him do it! There are no such extenuating circumstances.

- There is nothing wrong with **window-shopping**. And if we "walk with the Spirit" (Romans 7:25) we will keep it under control, and we will know when window-shopping becomes lust that leads to sin. As soon as we become aware that we have become obsessive and **must** have the item, we can make a decision to withdraw at that point. We do not have to allow (choice) the desire to become lust,

¹⁵Then, after desire has conceived, it gives birth to sin; and sin, when it is full-grown, gives birth to death.

James 1:15.

If however the choice is made to pursue the lust, then illegitimate and illegal processes may eventuate. The result could be stealing, or smashing the shop window in desperation to acquire the product. The final method is immaterial—it is sin.

This was the problem that **Achan** experienced:

>[21] When ***I saw*** *in the plunder a beautiful robe from Babylonia, two hundred shekels of silver and a wedge of gold weighing fifty shekels,* ***I coveted*** *them and* ***took*** *them.*
>
> Joshua 7:21, emphases added.

Achan permitted (choice) his desire to grow and produce fruit—*saw ... coveted ... took*—and it graphically ended in death—for him and his whole family and his possessions (Joshua 7:1-26). Note especially:

>[24] *Then Joshua, together with all Israel, took Achan son of Zerah, the silver, the robe, the gold wedge, his sons and daughters, his cattle, donkeys and sheep, his tent and all that he had, to the Valley of Achor.*
>[25] *Joshua said, "Why have you brought this trouble on us? The LORD will bring trouble on you today." Then all Israel stoned him, and after they had stoned the rest, they burned them.*
>[26] *Over Achan they heaped up a large pile of rocks ...*
>
> Joshua 7:24-26.

No "nature" made Achan covet and act so deceitfully. There is no "passing the buck". That was his choice, and he is responsible and culpable, and he was rightly held accountable.

2.3.3 BRIEF SCRUTINY OF GALATIANS 5.

**NOTE: PIVOTAL ISSUE #4:
'FLESH' IN GALATIANS 5. (See the Introduction).

Galatians 5 relating to the works of the flesh in particular, is very helpful in trying to understand the operation of the "flesh".

This pivotal passage, apart from the usage of flesh in the three Old Man passages below, is verses 16-25 (NKJV). The New King James version has been quoted to simplify the references to "flesh", because they are correctly rendered there.

¹⁶I say then: Walk in the Spirit, and you shall not fulfil the lust of the flesh.
¹⁷For the flesh lusts against the Spirit, and the Spirit against the flesh; and these are contrary to one another, so that you do not do the things that you wish.
¹⁸But if you are led by the Spirit, you are not under the law.
¹⁹Now the works of the flesh are evident, which are: adultery, fornication, uncleanness, lewdness,
²⁰idolatry, sorcery, hatred, contentions, jealousies, outbursts of wrath, selfish ambitions, dissensions, heresies,
²¹envy, murders, drunkenness, revelries, and the like; of which I tell you beforehand, just as I also told you in time past, that those who practice such things will not inherit the kingdom of God.
²²But the fruit of the Spirit is love, joy, peace, longsuffering, kindness, goodness, faithfulness,
²³gentleness, self-control. Against such there is no law.
²⁴And those who are Christ's have crucified the flesh with its passions and desires.
²⁵If we live in the Spirit, let us also walk in the Spirit.

A. THE WORKS OF THE FLESH (vv. 16-21).

Verse 16:

¹⁶I say then: Walk in the Spirit, and you shall not fulfil the lust of the flesh.

- "walk": *peripateō* (περιπατεω) The word is made up of *peri*, around, and *pateō*, to tread, and hence means literally "to walk around". It is the going to and fro of life, the normal round of activities.

  The verb is **present** active imperative, and therefore explains **continuity** of action. It is the act of continually conducting one's self or ordering one's manner of life, or behaviour. It is not too strong to state (**and it is a command**): "Habitually dwell under the influence of the Spirit and you will not consummate the strong cravings of the natural desires". See explanation of Greek tenses below.

- "you shall (not) fulfil": *teleō* (τελεω). Means to give effect to, to complete or perfect, bring to a conclusion, to carry out to the full. There is no attempt to deny the normal desires of the flesh, but like all temptation, it does not have to find fulfilment in an illicit extreme. We do not have to consummate the **lust** of the flesh—we are not under compulsion. There is no bypassing of our wills.

- "Spirit": *pneuma* (πνευμα) This can only be a reference to the Holy Spirit as is dictated by the context, noting especially the statement of verse 22: "fruit of the Spirit", as well as being used by way of comparison twice in verse 17.

- "not": *ou mē* (οὐ μη) Both words are negative, thus forming a "double negative". Hence the statement is emphatic in itself, but it is used with a verb that is aorist active subjunctive which gives the sense of a future indicative but with even more emphasis. There is absolutely no doubt—no way—that you will succumb to the natural desires of the flesh if you are walking with a consenting will with the Spirit. It is almost an impossibility (See re Joseph later). But you may—if you so choose. You never surrender your will.

- "the lust (of the flesh)": *epithumia* (ἐπιθμια). The combination of *epi,* upon or intensive, and *thumia,* strong passion, denotes emphatically strong passion. It is neutral in itself—as we see as it is applied to the Spirit in verse 17—but the context will indicate the direction it is going. Very often it is used in the bad sense. Earnest desire, irregular or strong desire.

- "the flesh": *sarx* (σαρξ). In the context of Galatians 5, the flesh is seen in the sense of a natural desire that is being pursued as an end in itself. This becomes clear in verses 19-21, where the "works of the flesh" portray the activity of the Christian in its aberrant form, q.v. Here it is shown by "lusts" or *strong desires* of the flesh—not just the flesh itself.

Verse 17:

¹⁷For the flesh lusts against the Spirit, and the Spirit against the flesh; and these are contrary to one another, so that you do not do the things that you wish.

- "flesh": *sarx* (σαρξ)   as for verse 16.

- "lusts": *epithumeō* (ἐπιθυμεω). This verb is related to the noun *epithumia* in verse 16. *Epi* + *thumeō* expressing intense passion. Of itself it is a neutral word. It is the present active indicative—again indicating continuity of action. While we are in the flesh we will never be released from the strong motivations—albeit natural—of the flesh. We will always be battling with the "bulge" as far as food is concerned, as also in other areas as well.

NOTE that the verb applies to both the flesh and the Spirit, and we need to note that **the word is neutral of itself.

- "and these are contrary to one another, so that you do not do the things that you wish": actually the translation should read: "these things (the flesh and the Spirit) are opposed to each other, lest you should do whatever you wish". The verb is: *antikeimai* (ἀντικειμαι). The word comes from *anti*, meaning against, and *keimai,* to lie, so that the word itself means "to lie opposite, to be set over against" (Vine *et al*, 1996, Vol. 2, 15). The extreme passions of the flesh are in direct opposition to the holy strivings of the Holy Spirit. But this is not a vacuum for the Christian. YOU still have to make a choice. The Holy Spirit is opposed to the **habitual sins** to which you have become accustomed, and the habits are experiences that you have yielded to and appreciated (or you would not have yielded), and there is a great tension, because you want to revisit these old evils.

But **you are never dominated or ruled by either party.**

- "you": not the "sin nature" or "the old nature" or any other personalised concept of an independent entity with determinative powers, but YOU. It is your choice.

- "lest you should do whatever **you wish**" (adapted). This is a purpose clause in the present tense (a subjunctive) expressing and emphasising continuity or repeated action. This is an *attempted* prohibition, not an *actual* prohibition. The ongoing tension between the habitual sins and the Holy Spirit are operating in a way that the Spirit is expressing strong passion against the habitual sins—to keep you back—but the habitual sins are so much part of your life that you don't want to let them go. But it's your choice. And "lest you should do whatever YOU wish"—and you can—but the Holy Spirit with your best interest at heart is strongly urging restraint. You are free to do right!

Verse 18:

¹⁸But if you are led by the Spirit, you are not under the law.

- "you are led": *agō* (ἀγω), to bear, carry, conduct, bring, lead. The verb is present passive indicative. If your ongoing (present continuous) position is one in which you have chosen to be led by the Spirit, then you are free. You are not under law.

- "under law". One might have expected Paul to have said, "You are not under the flesh". On the contrary, we are under grace. That does not give freedom to sin (as he noted in Romans 6:1), and having continually yielded to the Spirit, we will not want to sin.

Verse 19:

¹⁹Now the works of the flesh are evident, which are: adultery, fornication, uncleanness, lewdness,

- "works (of the flesh)": *ergon* (ἐργον). The natural energy of the flesh is to go to extreme, in the attempt to satisfy that basic need. Instead of enjoying food, we are gluttonous. How many times have I been to a smorgasbord restaurant, and come out feeling so uncomfortably bloated that I vow that I will never eat again! But there is no lasting satisfaction and I am ready to line up for breakfast next morning!

In the following list, Paul looks at the **extremes or aberrations** of many natural desires. It must be these extremes or unlawful acts that he is referring to, because **the Spirit is not opposed to that which He created—the *normal* desires of the flesh.**

- "evident": *phaneros* (φανερος), clear, evident, open to sight. It is perfectly obvious what the **works** of the flesh are, because they are all repulsive when looked at **objectively in their extreme presentation.**

- "adultery": *moicheia* (μοιχεια). There is nothing wrong with sex as God's good creation, as we have noted. But when we are not satisfied to fulfil that normal healthy desire in its proper bonds of marriage, and pursue it in an illegitimate way, then it is a serious problem.

- "fornication": *porneia* (πορνεια). This word covers a variety of immoral actions including bestiality, prostitution, and problems of consanguinity. It is illicit sex. Again, there is nothing wrong with sex, but when it is pursued as an end in itself without regard for God's good purpose, it becomes a sweaty (work) of the flesh that does not satisfy. It is sin.

- "uncleanness": *akatharsia* (ἀκαθαρσια), literally "not purified". In the papyri it is used of tenants not keeping their houses in good condition (Vine, *et al*, 1996). Of the 10 occurrences in the New Testament, at least half are related to moral uncleanness: lewdness, fornication, adultery, etc.

It is also used of uncleanness in relation to idolatry. Even at the most elementary level of failing to keep the house clean—it might be OK to drop your clothes on the floor as you go to bed, or to leave dirty dishes in the sink after breakfast—but when this becomes the way of life, then the landlord wants to have an inspection. And what is not satisfactory for the landlord is even more something against which the Holy Spirit has strong passion to oppose.

- "lewdness": *aselgeia* (ἀσελγεια), denotes "excess, licentiousness, absence of restraint, indecency, wantonness"; "lasciviousness" (Vine, *et al*, 1996, Vol. 2, 649). In 2 Peter 2:2 it refers to the filthy lives of those of Sodom and Gomorrah. The prominent idea is shameless conduct, outrageous behaviour, and insolent contempt of public opinion. The central thing is this lack of restraint and respect. Instead of good behaviour that is tempered and restrained, here is behaviour that is opposed to all that reflects the holy God we worship.

Verse 20:

[20]*idolatry, sorcery, hatred, contentions, jealousies, outbursts of wrath, selfish ambitions, dissensions, heresies,*

Reminder: these are **lusts** of the flesh—extremes—the counterpart of the normal and natural. They are illegal or inappropriate behaviours that are contrary to God's holiness, and are therefore strongly opposed by the Holy Spirit.

- "idolatry": *eidōlolatria* (ειδωλολατρια) It is fundamental to man to worship, and there is nothing wrong with that, but if this becomes an obsession with anything, or person, or personal goal, etc., it becomes idolatry. Becoming a slave to depraved ideas represented by idols, or the god(s) they represent.

- "sorcery": *pharmakeia* (φαρμακεια), from this we can see the transliteration "pharmacy"—the use of drugs and medicine. There is nothing wrong with medicine in its correct usage, but when it becomes hallucinogenic and addictive and other drugs used for illegitimate purposes, accompanied by incantations appealing to occult powers, together with poisoning and sorcery, there is a problem.
- "hatred": *echthra* (ἐχθρα). There is nothing wrong with friendly rivalry, but when this becomes a state of hostility, of discord, feud, enmity and personal animosity, it is the sweaty "work of the flesh".
- "contentions": *eris* (ἐρις). There is nothing wrong with holding a particular personal viewpoint, but if that becomes a cause of altercation, strife, contentious disposition, leading to the expression of enmity, debate and rivalry, then we have the normal being pursued to an unhealthy and unhelpful extreme. That is sin (cf. "selfish ambition").
- "jealousies": *zēlos* (ζηλος). The transliteration "jealousy" is evident from the Greek. There is nothing wrong with having aspirations and goals—indeed we should have them—but when we become jealous of others and their goals and successes, then there is indignation, wrath, and unfriendly feeling with malice—the lust of the flesh.
- "outbursts of wrath": *thumos* (θυμος). There is nothing wrong with being passionate about anything—indeed we often fail to be sufficiently passionate about things and issues that really matter—but if this is the expression resulting from jealousy or rivalry, there is a problem. The Greek word expresses explosive emotions, uncontrolled temper, emotions which quickly blaze up and equally quickly subside. It is used of Herod's reaction when he heard that a child had been born in his jurisdiction who was a king (Matthew 2:16).

- "selfish ambitions": *eritheia* (ἐριθεια). Again (many of these words are simply shades of variation from each other cf. "contentions" above), there is nothing wrong with ambition and setting goals, but if that becomes selfish ambition, self-will leading to faction-making, self-seeking leading to contentious rivalry, there is much sweat and strife—the **work** of the flesh.

- "dissensions": *dichostasia* (διχοστασια). The word itself is made up of two parts: *dichē* – asunder or apart, and *stasis* – a standing. Literally "a standing apart". There is nothing wrong with making a stand to oppose evil, to be holy in standing apart from or separate from sinful practices and/or people, but if this is the cause of dissension in the fellowship, dissecting and causing division, then this is the work of the devil.

- "heresies": *haireseis* (αἱρεσεις). Again, the transliteration is obvious from the Greek: heresies. There is nothing wrong with holding opinions—the root word for heresies is a word meaning "to choose"—to make a choice, but if that becomes a self-willed opinion that is held and causes factions and strife, then it is counterproductive to the fellowship and God's work. The Spirit is strongly opposed to that.

Such animosity leads to dislike, not only of others' points of view, but also of the others themselves. Peter warns of this type of heretical behaviour (2 Peter 2:1-2, emphasis added):

> [1]*But there were also false prophets among the people, just as there will be false teachers among you. They will secretly introduce **destructive heresies**, even denying the sovereign Lord who bought them—bringing swift destruction on themselves.*
> [2]*Many will follow their shameful ways and will bring the way of truth into disrepute.*

Verse 21:

²¹envy, murders, drunkenness, revelries, and the like; of which I tell you beforehand, just as I also told you in time past, that those who practice such things will not inherit the kingdom of God.

- "envy": *phthonos* (φθονος). There is nothing wrong with ambition (cf. previously) and friendly rivalry, but when competition results in the feeling of displeasure produced by witnessing or hearing of the advantage or prosperity of others, then there is a begrudging attitude that is sinful. The stoics defined it as "grief at someone else's good" (Barclay 1958, 53).

- "murders": *phonos* (φονος). Although this is a textual variant to "envy"—note the similarity of the Greek words—it is still relevant. Not that there is a "normal" counterpart to this item, unless one is speaking of "putting to death" the practices of the body, but we would still not use "murder". It seems to be the extreme of envyings and dissensions, and is the final outcome of these evils. The word itself can convey the idea of "slaughter".

- "drunkenness": *methē* (μεθη). Whilst the use of wine, almost always diluted—from two parts of water to twenty parts of water with one part of wine—certainly as a protection against amoebic dysentery or otherwise with impure water systems—was almost a necessity in those cultures, it would take an extreme abuse of the product, which under normal circumstance would affect the bladder long before it would affect the mind! Any abuse was disgraceful and unwarranted at every level. Although alcohol was beneficial in right proportion, it required temperance in order to maintain that balance.

- "revelries": *kōmos* (κωμος). There is nothing wrong with having a party or celebrating, but when "partying" becomes an all-consuming obsession, as is common in our modern society, there becomes a problem with excesses—excessive feasting, carousing, drinking parties, unrestrained and uncontrolled revelry. Enjoyment that degenerates into licence. A *kōmos* was a band of friends who accompanied a victor of the games after his victory, associated with *excesses* (Barclay 1958, 53).

- "and the like": The list thus far is not exhaustive! But we have covered sufficient examples to indicate Paul's concern about the illegal, illegitimate, sensuous, etc., attempt to fulfil or pursue natural normal appetites in the wrong way. Of themselves they are OK, but pursued as an end in themselves, they are sinful.

- "just as I also told you": as far as the Galatians are concerned, Paul has already addressed these issues with them before.

- "(those who) practice": *prassō* (πρασσω), to do in the sense of practicing. Again Paul reinforces that he is not addressing the normal, but the aberrant—things that are not only wrong in themselves, but are **practiced** continually. A Christian may commit sin, but he would not **practice** these things. These practitioners will not inherit the kingdom of God.

B . THE FRUIT OF THE SPIRIT (vv. 22-25)

²²But the fruit of the Spirit is love, joy, peace, longsuffering, kindness, goodness, faithfulness,
²³gentleness, self-control. Against such there is no law.
²⁴And those who are Christ's have crucified the flesh with its passions and desires.
²⁵If we live in the Spirit, let us also walk in the Spirit.

The "fruit of the Spirit" gives a strong contrast to the "works of the flesh". Although they are the natural "outcropping" of the Holy Spirit, they are still dependent on being fulfilled by our consenting will. The Spirit does not produce this fruit independently of us. He does not dominate us. And we can never abdicate to the Holy Spirit and say, "You'll have to love him/her because I can't".

We can refuse to love someone, and so inhibit the Spirit's operation. We thus yield to the lust of the flesh by demonstrating bitterness or hatred or envy, instead of love. Are we willing to love the given person, or are we willing to be longsuffering or patient? In all situations we are involved.

The final alternative operation in our bodies will be according to our **consenting wills**—whether it is to be the lust of the flesh, or the fruit of the Spirit. Just as Paul noted in Romans 6:16 (emphases added):

*[16]Don't you know that when you **offer yourselves** [**consenting will**] to someone to obey him as slaves, you are slaves to the one whom you obey—**whether you are slaves to sin**, which leads to death, **or to obedience**, which leads to righteousness?*

I am totally responsible for my actions.

Verse 23:

[23]gentleness, self-control. Against such there is no law.

- "against such there is no law". Keeping the law is not limited to only doing, or avoiding those things prescribed in the law. Some things cannot be legislated for—for example mercy and grace. And yet those were the very intentions of the law.

The prophet Micah made this clear, stating that in spite of the law the real requirements were what God has shown them:

> *[8]He has showed you, O man, what is good. And what does the LORD require of you? **To act justly and to love mercy and to walk humbly** with your God.*
>
> Micah 6:8, emphasis added.

When Jesus remonstrated against the teachers of the law and the Pharisees, he said, *inter alia*,

> *²³ ... But you have neglected the **more important matters of the law—justice, mercy and faithfulness** ...*
>
> Matthew 23:23, emphases added.

Therefore, things like the fruit of the Spirit, although not part of the legal code, should not be ignored. Producing such fruit will not in fact break the law, even if it does not specifically fulfil the law, yet it is the manifestation of a life right with God. Certainly Jesus clearly stated that the first of the fruit, love, **is** the fulfilling of the law.

> *³⁷Jesus replied: " '**Love** the Lord your God with all your heart and with all your soul and with all your mind.'*
> *³⁸This is the first and greatest commandment.*
> *³⁹And the second is like it: '**Love** your neighbour as yourself.'*
> *⁴⁰**All the Law and the Prophets hang on these two commandments.**"*
>
> Matthew 22:37-40, emphases added.

Paul likewise exhorted that love was the fulfilling of the law:

> *⁸Let no debt remain outstanding, except the continuing debt to love one another, for **he who loves his fellowman has fulfilled the law.***
> *¹⁰Love does no harm to its neighbour. Therefore **love is the fulfilment of the law.***
>
> Romans 13:8, 10, emphases added.

In Galatians 5:18, in the context of the works of the flesh, Paul stated: *if you are led by the Spirit, you are not under the **law**.* The law has no bearing on the fruit of the Spirit, in the same way as the law has no bearing on being led by the Spirit.

Verse 24:

²⁴And those who are Christ's have crucified the flesh with its passions and desires.

- "have crucified the flesh". This is an ingressive aorist, indicating that a state—in this case of death—has been entered into, with regard to the flesh, in a similar way to the crucifixion of the Old Man.

  We are now commanded to deal with the limbs, since we have already dealt with the trunk of the tree. See later in #5.4 LIFE UNDER GRACE, in Colossians.

  The Christian does not **go on fulfilling** (continuous) the lusts of the flesh, even if he does occasionally sin. Because all the desires of the natural man are natural and normal, they will still be with him while he is in the body. Sex does not go away because you are a Christian. Appetite for food does not disappear upon conversion. And your reference point is the behaviour in the past. If **habitually** you indulged in any passion, then that habit will still be inculcated in the body, and there will be a learning process to rectify it—see Chapter 5 particularly.

Verse 25:

²⁵If we live in the Spirit, let us also walk in the Spirit.

- "if we live". The Greek construct is a fulfilled condition, and therefore the translation should be: "**Since** we live in the Spirit". Since we are Christians. This is our present situation. That being the case, let us walk in a way that reflects that position.

- "walk (in the Spirit)": *stoicheō* (στοιχεω). As distinct from the word for "to walk" in verse 16 (*peripateō*), *stoicheō* means to follow, be in line with, hold to, agree, walk in step with. Hence the need to "frame one's conduct", to be consistent with—in this case the Holy Spirit.

Since we are Christians, then let us make sure that we live according to that standard. WE have to consent to that—it is an operation of the will to the power and enabling of the Holy Spirit.

C. SUMMARY: there are several things to note carefully.

1. **The flesh is normal** and God created it with basic desires and appetites.

2. The **desires** and **lusts** of the flesh, as demonstrated in Galatians 5, are the legitimate passions of the flesh but taken to illegitimate extremes that constitute them sinful.

3. At every stage, the operation of the flesh is ONLY with the **consenting will. We never abdicate the will.**

4. The need for the Christian is to act with a **consenting will to the Holy Spirit** Who passionately opposes the lusts of the flesh for our best interests.

5. The biggest problem with this whole operation is that of behaviours that have become **habits** at any stage, and which have therefore developed patterns—that by-pass the will—and expected appetites that we have learned to assume. If we go to a restaurant it might be automatic to "eat to the full" without thinking about the aspects of gluttony or self-control. These must be addressed.

2.4 LEARNED BEHAVIOUR (AS A CHRISTIAN)

It is learned behaviour (or any other learned thing for that matter) that usually results in automatic responses that are called **habit reactions**. We have noted this problematic area as we addressed the tension between the works of the flesh and the fruit of the Spirit.

We have also noted that these develop naturally in the non-Christian state under the Old Man. It becomes "normal" as a non-Christian to lose one's temper, "normal" to react angrily with other motorists and to indulge in "road-rage", to swear when things don't go as one wants, to lie to advance one's interests for promotion, and the list goes on. Whilst it is not desirable, let alone acceptable behaviour, nevertheless it is understandable in the non-Christian state under the Old Man condition, with Satan as the boss.

We will look at the matter of rectifying this behaviour in the Christian walk in Chapter 5, but for the moment let us note that the habit responses of the non-Christian condition can also be developed in the Christian state under the New Man.

It is all to do with **the will**.

If as a Christian, we succumb to temptation and steal from the boss—of course only small items of stationary, or a few nails and bolts on the building site—it soon becomes a way of life, and there is a regular "sampling" of products. This can become a habit without any immediate guilt attached to it. And without thinking about it as we do it.

This can happen in the area of attitudes as well. I remember talking to a couple of ladies after the Ladies' Bible Study. They both had non-Christian husbands and were making excellent progress in their Christian walk without any support from home. As they chatted on, I was a little alarmed as they shared that they no longer felt the "wrong" of illicit relationships as they had felt upon conversion. I listened as I tried to ascertain if there was some reason for this change.

Suddenly one of the ladies looked at her watch, "Oh, I must get going—or I'll miss 'Days of Our Lives'" (or whatever the soapie was). The other lady agreed, as they hastily left. The answer to their problem was immediately evident. The regular uncritical watching of unprincipled soapies, with a constant line of illicit relationships, had led them to become quite blasé about the principles of God's Word, and indifferent to these shallow and unprincipled relationships.

Without consenting to any actual behaviour themselves, nevertheless they were consenting to the behaviour they were watching, and in the relaxed mood of being entertained, they had lost their Christian convictions in that area at least.

We just note the fact that the development of habits is not limited to the domain of the Old Man state. And we need to be vigilant as Christians. We still have consenting wills. Beware to what we consent.

> [16]*Don't you know that when you* ***offer yourselves*** *[consenting will]* ***to someone to obey*** *him as slaves, you are slaves to the one whom you obey—whether you are slaves to sin, which leads to death, or to obedience, which leads to righteousness?*
> [17]*But thanks be to God that, though* ***you used to be slaves to sin****, you wholeheartedly obeyed the form of teaching to which you were entrusted.*
> [18]*You have been* ***set free from sin*** *and have become* ***slaves to righteousness.***
>
> Romans 6:16-18, emphases added.

* * * * *

CHAPTER 3

THE OLD MAN

NOTE: PIVOTAL ISSUE #5: THE OLD MAN. (See the book Introduction).

3.1 INTRODUCTION

The Old Man is a term only occurring **three times** in the Bible. It is a very important concept theologically, but this has been lost by incorrect translation (see tables at #3.4.1: TRANSLATIONS OF OLD MAN/NEW MAN, below).

The Old Man is the condition of unregenerate humanity, identified in union with Adam. It is our condition naturally after our corporate sin in Adam (on this corporate sin, see the earlier volume *Condemned Already*, Swincer 2011a). It is not a reference to our nature as if it were some part of us. It is not a person with a will. It is not an abstract principle—an abstract principle cannot be responsible for a sin a man commits.

All too commonly the Old Man is spoken of as the "sinful nature".

Rather, "It is the unregenerate ego with all its ramifications through the whole of human life" (Gibson n.d., 1).

Subsequently, after the corporate sin in Adam and the development of the Old Man condition, anyone accepting Christ and receiving salvation, puts on the New Man—the new life in Christ.

The Old Man and the New Man are intrinsically related to the two Adams.

> ⁴⁵*So it is written: "The **first man Adam** became a living being" the **last Adam**, a life-giving spirit.*
> ⁴⁶*The spiritual did not come first, but the natural, and after that the spiritual.*
> ⁴⁷*The **first man** was of the dust of the earth, the **second man** [Adam] from heaven.*
>
> 1 Corinthians 15:45-47, emphases added.

We also note that each one of us has a significant **identification** factor with the two Adams:

> ²²*For as **in Adam** all die, so **in Christ** [the second Adam] all will be made alive.*
>
> 1 Corinthians 15:22, emphases added.

This identification was developed in *Condemned Already* (Swincer 2011a), and is basic to our understanding of our condition as sinners, involving personal responsibility and culpability.

3.2 THE OLD MAN—IN THREE PASSAGES

3.2.1 ROMANS 6:6

> ⁶*For we know that **our old self** (sic) was crucified with him so that the body of sin might be done away with, that we should no longer be slaves to sin*

- "our": *hēmōn* (ἡμων). Obviously this is a plural pronoun. The significant thing is that it is connected to a singular noun—"man". Hence it is "our collective".

- "old": *palaios* (παλαιος): "of what is of long duration, old in years," of that which was given long ago and remains in force, that which was familiar and well known in contrast to that which is fresh (*kainos,* καινος) (Vine, *et al*, 1996,

Vol. 2, 430-431). There are two words in the Greek for "old", see the following.

**NOTE: re the two words for "old".

Palaios denotes "old," "without the reference to beginning and origin contained in *archaios*" (Abbott-Smith), a distinction observed in the papyri (Moulton and Milligan). While sometimes any difference seems almost indistinguishable, yet "it is evident that wherever an emphasis is desired to be laid on the reaching back to a beginning, whatever that beginning may be, *archaios* will be preferred (e.g., of Satan, Rev. 12:9; 20:2). That which ... is old in the sense of more or less worn out ... is always *palaios*" (Trench).

Vine, et al, 1996, Vol. 2, 444.

The application of *palaios* to the Old Man as the condition outside of Christ, is not related to antiquity so much as to that which is worn out and ready to be discarded. It is our condition with an unregenerated ego. And it is **held collectively with all mankind**—all who were unregenerated outside of Christ.

It is this **collective factor** in particular that is lost when we fail to translate correctly using the (**our**) Old Man.

In particular, the **collective** relationship between the first Adam and the last Adam is lost in the particular context of sin. Our (collective sin together with)—as *participants*, not with Adam as a *representative*—is lost. We (collectively) have sinned in Adam, and we (collectively) have been crucified with Christ.

This relationship is emphasized and clarified in 1 Corinthians 15:22 (as just noted above):

> *²²For as in Adam all die, so in Christ* [the second Adam] *all will be made alive.*

This is the fundamental IDENTIFICATION aspect of the concept of Original Sin. See *Condemned Already* (Swincer 2011a).

- "man": *anthrōpos* (ἀνθρωπος) (Verse 6). This is the generic word for "mankind"—as opposed to *anēr* (man—as distinct from woman) and *gunē* (woman). In the singular here, and associated with the plural "our", it is a collective word.

  The Bible is speaking of *hēmōn palaios anthrōpos*, "our Old Man". This is NOT "the old self", and certainly not some "old nature"—a concept foreign to the New Testament. Although it is true that there is a difference in the ego before and after conversion—and hence the contrast of "old self/new self" is understandable—but the solidarity with Christ is lost, as well as solidarity with Adam.

  Of course, what is true *collectively*—**OUR** Old Man—that **we** have been crucified with Christ, is also true *individually*. **I** am crucified with Christ:

  > [20]*I have been crucified with Christ* and I no longer live, but Christ lives in me. The life I live in the body, I live by faith in the Son of God, who loved me and gave himself for me.

  Galatians 2:20, emphasis added.

  And this identification continues into the future:

  > [8]Now if we died with Christ, we believe that **we will also live WITH him.**

  Romans 6:8, emphasis added.

- "was crucified": *sunestaurōthē* (συνεσταυρωθη), is from the root *sustauroō*; *su-* elided for *sun*, "with"; plus *stauroō* signifying the act of crucifixion—"crucified together with". The composite word is used of (a) actual "crucifixion" **in company with** another, and (b) metaphorically, of spiritual **identification with** Christ in His death (Vine, *et al*, 1996, Vol. 2, 138)—and this is the usage here in this verse.

  The verb is aorist passive indicative, indicating that this was **a single act at a point in time in the past, never to be**

repeated. THE OLD MAN IS DEAD—NEVER TO RISE AGAIN. It is a once for all completed act. But **death is not extinction or annihilation, but it is separation and non-operation.**

Hence the "theology of the Grandfather's clock":

> **But it stopped short**
> **Never to go again,**
> **When the old man died.**

****NOTE**: the purpose of the death of our old man is:

1) To put on the New Man, and

2) *... that the body of sin might be done away with, that we should no longer be slaves to sin.* (Romans 6:6).

See further in Chapter 5.

3.2.2 EPHESIANS 4:21-22.

[21] Surely you heard of him and were taught in him in accordance with the truth that is in Jesus.
*[22] You were taught, with regard to your former way of life, to put off **your old self** (sic), which is being corrupted by its deceitful desires;*

Exactly as in Romans 6, we are dealing with the *palaios anthrōpos*—the Old Man—NOT some "old self" or "corrupt nature".

At first sight it appears that Ephesians is at variance with the other two passages that refer to the Old Man—Romans and Colossians. They both indicate past tense using the aorist. They both indicate completed acts in the past.

It is quite obvious that one cannot speak of a completed act, other than in the past. Hence in reference to the Old Man, Ephesians cannot be suggesting something that is either incomplete or future. Gibson comments:

Note the Greek construction of Eph. 4:22/24. Three verbs are infinitives, two are aorist – (ἀποθεσαι, put away, put off) – (ἐνδυσασθαι, put on, clothe oneself) and one is present – (ἀνανεουσθαι, passive of renew). Thus the Greek is not in the imperative, the normal mood of command. All the versions listed [see below] put these three Greek infinitives into English commands. But both J.H. Moulton (*Grammar of N.T. Greek*, 3:78) and A.T. Robinson (*Grammar of the Greek N.T.* p. 1078) indicate that the N.T. uses very rarely the infinitive in an imperative sense. By contrast frequently the Greek infinitive is used in an explanatory (epexegetical) clause. Thus we can say Eph. 4:22/24 are an enlargement of, or explanation of, **the truth as it is in Jesus**. And the truth of Jesus is always what **God has done**, not what we do. The passage thus correctly reads – "if you have heard of him and have been taught by him, even as is the truth in Jesus, namely, that **you have put off the old man** … you are being renewed … and that **you have put on the new man**."

Gibson n.d., 4, emphases added.

The Ephesian passage is thus explaining the truth in Jesus (verse 21), noting that the old man has already been "put off", and the new man has been "put on". **Truth is only ever in the past and is completed!**

Hoekema (1987, 80) like Gibson, explains the Ephesian passage referring to "explanatory infinitives", indicating that they are explanatory of the "truth as it is Jesus", that in fact they had no need to live longer like the Gentiles because—as they had been taught—"they have put off the old self (sic) and have put on the new self (sic)". It is a completed act.

But **note**, the putting off did not occur by an act of our will, but by the Old Man being crucified with Christ as Romans 6:6 indicated.

- "your (old self [man])" (verse 22). The Old Man is related to "your", *humas* (ὑμας), which is the pronoun for "you", but it is in the plural. Like Romans 6:6, the Old Man is related to a corporate condition, a plural *pronoun* ("you"—plural) with the singular *noun*—"man".

3.2.3 COLOSSIANS 3:9.

⁹*Do not lie to each other, since you have taken off your old self* (sic) *with its practices.*

Exactly as in Romans 6, and Ephesians 4, we are dealing with the *palaios anthrōpos,* NOT some "old self".

- "taken off", *apekdusamenoi* (ἀπεκδυσαμενοι). The root is *apekdusomai;* from *apo* "away from", plus *ekduō*. In turn *ekduō* is from *ek* "from, out of", plus *dunō* "to sink, go down" (Bagster, n.d., 108). The combined meaning is "to strip off, take off, unclothe; to renounce" (Bagster, n.d. 123) and the prefix *apo* conveys the perfective sense: "to strip clean off" (Robertson, 1931, 502). This has been a thorough operation. The Old Man has completely and utterly gone—of that there is no doubt. Not annihilated, but rendered completely ineffective.

  The verb is aorist **middle**, indicating a reflex action that took place at a point in time in the past, and is complete, never to be repeated. **The use of the aorist is determinative.** There has been a complete and thorough removal of the Old Man. But as noted above, it is not an act achieved by the operation of the will, even if it is reflexive, but it is accomplished by "crucifixion" (Romans 6:6).

- "your (old self)", is not actually in the Greek but it is implied because the verb dominating this verse is in the second plural (you)—*pseudesthe* (ψευδεσθε): "(You) do not lie ...".

- "with [his] practices", *sun autou tais praxesin* (συν αὐτου ταις πραξεσιν). The practices, or habits, that were generated in the Old Man condition have been put off together with the Old Man. The problem still remains, that the *patterns* of these habits are still embedded in the flesh, and that means that they can recur. There has to be a whole new learning and "repatterning" in order to address this issue. See table below at #3.4.1.

3.3 THE NEW MAN—IN THREE PASSAGES

3.3.1 INTRODUCTION

The same aberrations in translation occur with the counterpart to the Old Man, namely the New Man. (See the table below). Just as the biblical term *palaios anthrōpos* for the Old Man is not translated as such in any translation, except the Authorised Version, Young's Literal Translation, and once in Phillips', so also *kainos (neos) anthrōpos*—the New Man, is not translated as such except for the AV, Young's Literal Translation, and once in Phillips'. (See table below at #3.4.1).

The New Man is the regenerated person in Jesus Christ. Galatians 3:27 says (emphasis added):

> [27]*for all of you who were baptized into Christ have* **clothed yourselves with Christ.**

- "Clothed" yourselves with Christ—"put on" Christ.

So also Romans 13:14 (emphasis added):

> [14]*Rather,* **clothe yourselves with the Lord Jesus Christ,** *and do not think about how to gratify the desires of the sinful nature (sic)* [flesh].

**NOTE: putting on (being clothed with) Christ is one thing, but there is the issue of what to do about the sinful practices. These require an operation of the will: see Chapter 5.

We will now look at this concept of the New Man in the three passages that talk about the Old Man—but first a clarification:

3.3.2 NOTE: THE TRANSITION: OLD →NEW

The transfer from the Old Man state to the New Man state does not involve some inert period. There is an immediate changeover. One does not wear two sets of clothes at the same time (Hoekema 1987, 80). Just as in changing one's clothes, the old are taken off and the clean ones are put on, and there is no appreciable interim gap, so there is a smooth transition from being a non-Christian and immediately becoming a Christian: putting off the Old Man and putting on the New Man.

Believers "are not, as has often been taught, both old selves (sic) and new selves (sic) but are indeed new selves (sic) in Christ" (Hoekema 1987, 81).

Stibbs (1959, 53) speaks of the Old Man (erroneously as the "sinful nature", and he makes the terms interchangeable) that it "must come under judgment". This makes the Old Man and the New Man contemporaneous—not the biblical position. The Old Man is crucified with Christ in a once-off past completed act.

Stibbs seeks to strengthen (or explain) his position by an allegorical approach, by reference to the Jewish race (51-59). He speaks of an old Israel and a new Israel—again something that does not have foundation in Scripture. Supposedly they exist contemporaneously and so the parallel is made with the Old and New Men being contemporaneous. Not true.

Criswell states: "the old heart of sin and the old nature of depravity **are still with us**" (137, emphasis added). This is then identified with the "passions" which he says are still with us, and which are a constant "drag". (How? The flesh has no identity or existence or will.) For him, there is no transition. The old condition still obtains. Actually the Bible makes it perfectly clear that the Old Man is crucified WITH its deeds, and that we are human beings with normal basic drives and appetites that do not have to be taken to any extreme that renders them as sin, and they are operated by the consent of our wills as unified persons—psychosomatic unities.

This truth is clearly stated in 2 Corinthians 5:17:

*[17]Therefore, if anyone is in Christ, he is a **new creation**; the **old has gone**, the **new has come**!*

- "the old (has gone)", *archaia* (ἀρχεια): "original, ancient" (from *archē*, ἀρχη, "a beginning": English, "archaic," "archaeology," etc.) While sometimes any difference seems almost indistinguishable with *palaios*—as used in **Old** Man—yet "it is evident that wherever an emphasis is desired to be laid on the reaching back to a beginning, whatever that beginning may be, *archaios* will be preferred (e.g., of Satan, Rev. 12:9; 20:2, …). That which … is old in the sense of more or less worn out … is always … *palaios*" (Trench). (Vine, *et al*, 1996, Vol. 2, 444).

The Old Man describes the condition, but the **old** as a totality of when we commenced life, has now gone—rendered inactive, not annihilated.

- "(the old) has gone", *parēlthen* (παρηλθεν), is in the aorist, indicating a completed action at a point of time in the past.

** The old life has gone, finished (aorist), just as the Old Man is dead—aorist—never to rise again. This is consistent with our conversion experience. Sometime in the past we made a commitment to Christ, and that was the conclusion of that old condition—our pre-conversion life.

The aorist here gives a definitive statement about our salvation. The completed act is completed!! It is not reversible. We can conclude that our salvation is effected and is not reversible. "Once saved always saved".

- "the new (has come)", *kaina* (καινα), new denotes "new," of that which is unaccustomed or unused, not "new" in time, recent, but "new" as to form or quality, of different nature from what is contrasted as old (Vine, *et al*,1996, Vol. 2, 430-431). *Kainos* is distinguished from another word for "new" *veos*, which signifies "new" in respect of time, that which is recent (Vine, *et al*,1996, Vol. 2, 256). Moule (1973, 482) questions to what degree this distinction can be made, but it is not critical, and there is some value in the minimal differentiation.

If I had an old Ford car, and got a *veos* car, irrespective of make or model, it would be the latest edition—new in the sense of recency. If however I bought a *kainos* car, it would be a brand new car, but it may be ten years old, or last year's model—new in sense of quality. And it would be a Ford!

In 2 Corinthians 5:17, the emphasis is on the "new" life as that which is new in form or quality—*kainos*. It is not just a new replacement of the old, and therefore the same type of life, even if more recent or up-to-date. It is new in the sense of totally different—of a different quality.

The AV translates: *all things are become new*. This is the new life in Christ.

Neos and *kainos* are sometimes used of the same thing, but there is a difference. In referring to the New Man,

> the 'new man' in Eph. 2:15 (*kainos*) is 'new' in differing in character ... but the 'new man' in Col. 3:10 (*neos*) stresses the fact of the believer's 'new' experience, recently begun, and still proceeding. "The old man in him ... dates as far back as Adam; a new man has been born, who therefore is fitly so called"
>
> Vine, *et al*, 1996, Vol. 2, 431.

- "(the new) has come", *gegonen* (γεγονεν), from *ginomai* "to be, become". All things have **become** new. The significant thing is that *gegonen* is in the perfect tense. We have noted that the aorist tense is "punctiliar"—a point in time in the past, and completed. The perfect tense indicates something that happened at a point in time in the past, **but with ongoing results that are observable now** (see further explanation below).

This is also consistent with our conversion experience. It is an accomplished fact. At some time in the past—indeed when we accepted Christ—we put on the new life in Christ (a completed act), but this has continuing evidence into the present and hopefully on into the future—growth in Christ.

The perfect tense, not only tells us that the action is complete, but that there are ongoing ramifications. This is consistent with the process of **sanctification**. The **fact** of conversion (in the past) is presently evidenced by the ongoing changed life, and the growth in grace.

Murray states the position very well, and a few more theologians would do well to take note:

> The old man is the unregenerate man; the new man is the regenerate man created in Christ Jesus unto good works. **It is no more feasible to call the believer a new man and an old man, than it is to call him a regenerate man and an unregenerate. And neither is it warranted to speak of the believer as having in him the old man and the new man**. This kind of terminology is without warrant and it is but another method of doing prejudice to the doctrine which Paul was so jealous to establish when he said, "Our old man has been crucified".
>
> Murray cited in Hoekema 1987, 81, emphases added.

**NOTE: on the Greek tenses.

A brief comparison of three of the Greek tenses we have referred to, can be helpful.

a. **Aorist** – a completed action at a point in time in the past.

b. **Perfect** – a completed act in the past BUT with ongoing evidence.

c. **Present** – a continuing action from the past, evident presently, and continuing on into the future.

If we were to apply these three tenses to "sitting on a chair", then we could note the following:

a. **Aorist Tense**: "I sat on the chair" – I sat on the chair at a point in time in the past, it could have been yesterday morning, or it could have been a year ago, but the action was done and complete, and I am no longer sitting there.

b. **Perfect Tense:** "I sat on the chair" – I sat on the chair at a point in time in the past, it could have been yesterday morning, or it could have been a year ago, and although the action was at a point in time, and completed then, it was not complete in the sense that there are ongoing ramifications that are evidenced by the fact that I am still sitting there (or fallen in a heap but still in the chair!), although there is no definition of how long I will remain sitting on the chair.

c. **Present Tense:** "I sat on the chair", or more likely, "I am sitting on the chair". I was sitting on the chair sometime in the past, although there is no definition of how long I may have been sitting there, I am still sitting there in the present, and I will continue to sit there, but there is no definition of how long that will last. Hence the phrase is used: "present continuous", to explain this type of ongoing action.

3.3.3 LOOKING AT THE NEW MAN IN THE THREE PASSAGES

A. ROMANS 6.

There is no reference to the New Man specifically in Romans 6, but Paul certainly looks at the new life of the Christian after the death of the Old Man, and how we should be seeking to live. This will be looked at further in Chapter 5, LIFE UNDER THE NEW MAN.

B. EPHESIANS 4:23-27

²³to be made new in the attitude of your minds;
*²⁴and to put on the **new self** (sic), created to be like God in true righteousness and holiness.*
²⁵Therefore each of you must put off falsehood and speak truthfully to his neighbour, for we are all members of one body.
²⁶"In your anger do not sin": Do not let the sun go down while you are still angry,
²⁷and do not give the devil a foothold.

- "the new (self)": *kainos* (καινος). This is "new" in the sense of that which is unaccustomed or unused, not "new" in time, recent, but "new" as to form or quality, of different nature from what is contrasted as old—see detail above on 2 Corinthians 5:17. Compare the new, *neos*, in Colossians 3:9, below.

- "(the new) self": *anthrōpos* (ἀνθρωπος). This is the generic word for man in the sense of "mankind". It is not nature! This is the New Man in Christ Jesus.

  The New Man is new in character, not previously existing. This is in the same sense as we saw in 2 Corinthians 5:17. And the verses indicate the changes that are expected in this new condition, as we shall note in more detail in Chapter 5.

- "made new": *ananeousthai* (ἀνανεουσθαι). This word—for making new, renewal—is in the present tense (passive infinitive) which suggests a continuing process. It is not in the past as the above translation implies. This is consistent with the process of sanctification mentioned in relation to 2 Corinthians 5:17. The new man is dynamic, not static, with continual growth, renewal and transformation.

C. COLOSSIANS 3: 7-8, 10

⁷You used to walk in these ways, in the life you once lived.

⁸But now you must rid yourselves of all such things as these: anger, rage, malice, slander, and filthy language from your lips.
*¹⁰and have put on the **new self** (sic), which is being renewed in knowledge in the image of its Creator.*

- "new (self) (sic)", *neos* (νεος) ("self" = "man" is implied by the comparison, it is not in the Greek). As noted above *veos*, signifies "new" in respect of time, that which is recent (Vine, *et al*,1996, Vol. 2, 256). The other word for "new": *kainos*, denotes "new," of that which is unaccustomed or unused, not "new" in time, recent, but "new" as to form or quality, of different nature from what is contrasted as old (Vine, *et al*,1996, Vol. 2, 430-431). Further explanation of the distinction is noted above on 2 Corinthians 5:17.

- "being renewed": *anakainoō* (ἀνακαινοω), from *ana* "back", or "again", and *kainoō* "new", as per the previous note. It is a present active articular participle indicating an ongoing process of being renewed. Sanctification.

Hence we can conclude that in Colossians, Paul is seeking to emphasise the *recency* of this change of status from the Old to the New Man, whereas in Ephesians the emphasis is on the *character* of this New Man. There is nothing contradictory here, just a difference of emphasis.

3.4 TRANSLATIONS OF OLD/NEW MAN

3.4.1 OLD MAN

It is regrettable that most translations fail to translate literally, and tend to be interpretative, almost paraphrasing these terms, and in so doing unwittingly conveying some significant effects on our theology. In my books on Tongues, Volumes 1 and 2 (see Swincer 2011b and 2016a), I have noted this serious ramification for the mistranslation of "tongues" by "unknown tongues", "tongues of ecstasy", etc. that convey something that

	ROM. 6:6	EPH. 4:22	COL. 3:9
AV	**old man**	**old man**	**old man**
RSV	old self	old nature	old nature
NEB	the man you once were	old human nature	old nature
CBW	former self	old self	old self
LB	old evil desires	old evil nature	old life
NAS	old self	old self	old self
NASB	old self	old self	old self
GNB	old being	old self	old self
ESV	old self	old self	old self
NIV	old self	old self	old self
PHIL	old selves	old way of living	**old man**
JB	former selves	old self	old self
YOU	**old man**	**old man**	**old man**

↑ OLD MAN
↓ NEW MAN   (See below for abbreviations)

	EPH. 4:22	COL. 3:9
AV	**new man**	**new man**
RSV	new nature	new nature
NEB	new nature	new nature
CBW	new self	new self
LB	new nature	new kind of life
NAS	new self	new self
NASB	new self	new self
GNB	new self	new self
ESV	new self	new self
NIV	new self	new self
PHIL	new life	**new man**
JB	new self	new nature
YOU	**new man**	**new (man)**

ABBREVIATIONS IN CHARTS:

CBW = C.B. Williams   JB = Jerusalem Bible

PHIL = Phillips' Trans'n   YOU = Young's Lit'l Trans'n

---

is not included in the texts, nor intended by the authors. We need to always translate literally in the first instance (Swincer 2015, 47-50, 55-59, 93-94).

It can be noted here that only the AV, Young's Literal Translation, and Phillip's on one occasion, that correctly translate *palaios anthrōpos* as Old Man (see the Charts).

3.4.2 NEW MAN

As for the Old Man, the same translation aberration exists, and only the AV, Young's Literal Translation, and Phillip's Translation (once) give the correct rendering.

3.4.3 WARNING

We have noted previously how that the "translation" of *palaios anthrōpos* as "old self" instead of as Old Man, loses the sense of the corporate sin in Adam, and results in a "nature" that is not a biblical position. Most significantly, the crucifixion of the Old Man is somehow lost. This is pivotal, because it is an aorist indicating a once for all completed act. Instead, most books speak of a nature (old or new, it seems to matter little, because there is some kind of continuity implied) that is quite different from the Old Man condition which has been annulled completely according to the biblical conditions.

We have already noted that **Stibbs** and **Criswell** speak of the two entities as coexisting.

A.J. Gordon states: " … sinning is one thing and a **sinful nature** (sic) is another; and we see **no evidence** in Scripture that the latter is **ever eradicated completely** while we are in the body." (1949, 118, emphasis added). Well there is clear evidence in Romans 6:6 that the "old man is crucified with Christ"—dead, rendered ineffective, finished—not annihilated or eradicated.

George Ingram says, "I (was) born with a **sinful nature** (sic)", and after becoming a Christian we find that "we are living a switchback life ... and the cause, the root of this matter, is that **sinful nature** (sic) with which we were born ..." (1964, 15). For Ingram, the sinful nature (sic) continues into our Christian experience. That is not the biblical position, even though Ingram's statement is prefaced by, "Now God's Word says plainly that the cause ... is the sinful nature (sic)..." (15). No, God's Word plainly does not say that.

A.S. Wilson makes the curious assertion, "Sin is the old nature (sic), unimprovable, 'past all cure', which has been called the root principle of evil, the flesh, the old self-life" (n.d. 66). Sin is neither the Old Man nor an "old nature", and yet Wilson wants to suggest that this "old nature" is to be "reckoned" by faith to be on the cross, and yet "it may exist with the new nature in the same life" (66). You can't have it both ways—on the cross and yet alive. This is a confusion of notions that really explains nothing.

But this idea of some type of co-existence is not uncommon. **Hoekema** (1987, 78) reports on the relation of these supposed two selves that was commonly held by Reformed theologians, that "the old self and the new self are distinguishable aspects of the believer". In this view, the Christian is partly a new self and partly an old self. Hoekema inaccurately uses the terms "old self" and "new self", rather than the correct terms "old man" and "new man".

He quotes one such author:

> The struggle [in the Christian life] ... is between the inner man of the heart ... and the old man who, though driven out of the centre, **still wants to maintain his existence**, and who fights

all the more fiercely the more territory he loses ... this is the struggle between two people in the same person ...

Cited in Hoekema 1987, 78, emphasis added.

By way of corrective, he refers to **John Murray**, who "takes vigorous exception to this understanding of the old and new self (sic)".

Murray states emphatically:

The contrast between the old man and the new man has frequently been interpreted as the contrast between that which is new in the believer and that which is old ... Hence the antithesis which exists in the believer between holiness and sin ... is the antithesis between the new man and the old man in him. The believer is both old man and new man; when he does well he is acting in terms of the new man which he is; when he sins he is acting in terms of the old man which he also still is. **This interpretation does not find support in Paul's teaching.**

Murray in Hoekema 1987, 79, emphasis added.

He goes on to say (as noted above), "**It is no more feasible to call the believer a new man and an old man, than it is to call him a regenerate man and an unregenerate**" (81).

I agree with Murray, as does Hoekema. There has been a changeover. The person in Christ is no longer the Old Man but the New Man—he is a new person. He is not—cannot be—both an Old Man and a New Man.

Regrettably Hoekema uses "self" instead of "man" (as does Murray), thus confusing the issue and negating some of his corrective argument.

He states clearly, that "we who are in Christ ... are no longer the old selves (sic) we once were" (79). More emphatically, the old state has gone. He then looks at Colossians 3:9-10 and points out that "you **have taken off** your old self (sic)" (emphasis added) noting that Paul is enjoining that the

Colossians were not *now (or daily)* taking off, but that they *have already done this*. It is a past act, and completed. He refers to the Greek participles that Paul uses—*apekdusamenoi* and *endusamenoi*—which are both aorist tense (noted earlier), thus describing "snapshot action" in the past.

Major Ian Thomas, in his book *The Saving Life of Christ,* (1964), even speaks of the "old man rearing his ugly head". How can that possibly be if he is *crucified with Christ*? That is a shameful commentary on his opinion of the effectiveness of the cross.

And so one could endlessly quote the confusion that reigns because of mistranslation in the first instance, and then a failure to perform careful exegesis in the second.

Collectively this should serve as a stern warning about the need to be careful in both translation and exegesis (see detail in Swincer 2015).

* * * * *

CHAPTER 4

CULPABILITY FOR SIN

4.1 INTRODUCTION

In *Condemned Already* we noted how easily Adam was blamed for what in fact was our personal CAUSATIVE sin.

We have noted that the focal point for sin, is the operation of the will—and that is personal. In the Old Man condition, the will is introverted—it is self-love.

We have also noted the operation of the will in #2.2. MOTIVATION FOR SIN, including **habit** sin, but recognising the difficulty with unwitting sin.

We now look at those three *motivations* of sin, in the context of the three *categories* of sin.

4.2 THREE CATEGORIES OF SIN

There are THREE CATEGORIES OF SIN—as an extension of "the operations of the will". This is typified in Psalm 19:12-14 (emphases added):

> [12] Who can discern his **errors**? Forgive my **hidden faults**.
> [13] Keep your servant also from **wilful sins**; may they not rule over me. Then will I be blameless, innocent of great transgression.
> [14] May the words of my mouth and the **meditation of my heart** be pleasing in your sight, O LORD, my Rock and my Redeemer.

Here the Psalmist identifies the three types of sin:

1. Unwitting/unconscious sins (verse 12)
2. Deliberate (wilful) sins (verse 13)
3. Sins as a result of the expression of the heart—habit sins (verse 14).

In explanation of the third type, note Jesus' words to the Pharisees and teachers:

> *³⁴You brood of vipers, how can you who are evil say anything good? For **out of the overflow of the heart the mouth speaks**. ³⁵The good man brings good things out of the good stored up in him, and the evil man brings evil things out of the evil stored up in him.*
>
> Matthew 12:34-35, emphasis added.

Jesus indicates that there are actions that proceed spontaneously from the heart. They are an automatic "overflow". Hence the Psalmist's words above: *May the ... **meditation of my heart** be pleasing in your sight, O LORD*. He knows that if the meditations of his heart are acceptable to God, then the words of his mouth will also be acceptable. They are the overflow. Hit your finger with a hammer, and an expletive will spontaneously issue, if that is the way you think—the meditation of the heart.

Let us look at the three categories of sin, and then note how they affect the personality (the mind, the emotions and the will), and this will help us to identify the problem Paul was experiencing as he wrote Romans 7:15-25—**A pivotal passage**.

Referring to the chart (below), we note each of the sins.

4.2.1 DELIBERATE SINS

When we sin deliberately—which is most of the time—the whole personality is involved.

The **mind** is involved, because we know that we are sinning, and we know that it is wrong. So we insert "Yes" in the chart.

The **will** is involved, because we are making a choice to sin, irrespective of our knowledge of it being wrong, that it offends against a holy God, even though it mocks the atoning work of Christ in dying for sin, and irrespective of the consequences of our actions. Again we insert "Yes".

Hence the **emotions** are also involved, and they are particularly hard and calloused, in that we can proceed without flinching in the face of God, or of knowing the consequences of our actions. And we insert a third "Yes".

Hence we have inserted a "Yes" at each part of the personality in the chart: (mind, emotions, and will).

PERSONALITY SIN	MIND	EMOTIONS	WILL
1. DELIBERATE	YES	YES	YES
2. UNINTENTIONAL	NO	NO	NO
3. HABIT	YES	??	NO

4.2.2 UNINTENTIONAL OR UNWITTING SINS

Referring to the example used earlier:

No doubt we have all had the experience of walking across a park in a city, only to find as we are stepping off the lawns to return to the footpath, that we notice a sign in the lawn (and facing the footpath)—not the direction from which we have just come—"DO NOT WALK ON THE GRASS". Too late!! Innocent but guilty!

Let us relate this experience to the aspects of personality in the chart.

The **mind** is not involved. As we walked innocently across the grass, we were perhaps happily whistling to ourselves. There was no malice in our action, no awareness that we were in fact infringing some local bylaw. There was nothing to be aware of. So we insert "No" in the chart above.

The **will** is not involved, because there was no choice in relation to the action. The fact of walking on the grass was not preceded by any decision to violate a bylaw, it was pure innocence. Again we insert "No".

By extension, the **emotions** are not involved in the offending action, although they may be *after* the prohibition sign is read. A third "No".

Hence we have inserted a "No" at each part of the personality aspects in the chart.

NOTE: We must bear in mind that even though the will was not actively involved, nevertheless we are responsible as if the will was active, and hence we are held responsible as we noted in the section in #2.2 MOTIVATION FOR SIN – when the will is neutral. It is nevertheless regarded as active.

4.2.3 HABIT SINS
(RELATE TO THE BY-PASSED WILL)

Referring to Paul's dilemma in the **pivotal chapter**, Romans 7:15-25 (see the book Introduction), let us recap that:

> [15] *I do not understand what I do. For what I want to do I do not do, but what I hate I do.*
> [16] *And if I do what I do not want to do, I agree that the law is good.*
> [17] *As it is, it is no longer I myself who do it, but it is sin living in me.*
> [18] *I know that nothing good lives in me, that is, in my sinful nature* (sic). *For I have the desire to do what is good, but I cannot carry it out.*

¹⁹For what I do is not the good I want to do; no, the evil I do not want to do—this I keep on doing.
²⁰Now if I do what I do not want to do, it is no longer I who do it, but it is sin living in me that does it.
²¹So I find this law at work: When I want to do good, evil is right there with me.
²²For in my inner being I delight in God's law;
²³but I see another law at work in the members of my body, waging war against the law of my mind and making me a prisoner of the law of sin at work within my members.
²⁴What a wretched man I am! Who will rescue me from this body of death?
²⁵Thanks be to God—through Jesus Christ our Lord! So then, I myself in my mind am a slave to God's law, but in the sinful nature a slave to the law of sin.

Here there is much confusion and distress for Paul.

The **mind** IS involved, because he says very clearly in verse 15 (and verse 19, q.v.) that there are things that he wants to do, therefore he knows exactly what they are—the mind is operative. Equally, in the same verse, there are things that he does not want to do, and he knows what they are. Hence we can say "Yes" in the chart identifying the mind in relation to habit sins.

The **will** IS NOT involved, because, although Paul has determination: *what **I want** to do I do not do, but what **I hate** I do*—he is expressing very strongly what he both wants and does not want—but he is not doing it. He is willing one thing, but his actions are doing the opposite. **The actions he performs** are not the result of the operation of the will. Hence we can say "No" in the chart in relation to the will for habit sins.

Clearly the **emotions** are in a "jangled" state. They are not hard as if he is indifferent to his actions, as was the case for the deliberate sins. They are not inert because there is no awareness of the situation and the defaulting action as with the unintentional sins. But Paul is in great distress, and he cries out:

> [24]*What a wretched man I am! Who will rescue me from this body of death?*
>
> Romans 7:24.

How to describe this situation? The emotions are involved in the sense that they are operating, but they are spectator to the tension unfolding, and reflect the stress of Paul in his dilemma. They are not cold and hard, they are not indifferent. They are confused. Hence we can insert "??" because there is no adequate description.

4.2.4 RESOLUTION of HABIT SINS

From an instructive point of view, it would have been better to have left the box entitled "HABIT" blank in the first instance. As we look at the characteristics of the sin as Paul experienced it in Romans 7, we could then ask the question, "What type of sin is described by the personality ramifications entered in the chart? What sin involves the **mind**, but bypasses the **will** and leaves the person's **emotions** in tension and distress?" The only answer is "**habit sins**".

It is an instructive exercise to reread the passage above (Romans 7:15-25) and to keep the awareness of habit sin in mind. **This is the only satisfactory explanation of Romans 7:15-25.** And this is a pivotal consideration in understanding the whole issue before us.

4.3 CULPABILITY IN ALL SITUATIONS

At no stage are we free of responsibility in terms of sins committed. In **all** situations we are to be held to account.

It matters not whether we sin deliberately, unintentionally, or habitually, we are responsible.

**NOTE:

1) **We are always responsible because we never surrender (nor can we) our wills.**

2) **There is never a third party "sinful nature", "flesh" or any other entity that can be personalised and give determination that over-rides our wills and responsibility.**

3) **Whoever we may have sinned against in any way, ultimately we are accountable to God, and therefore we can never seek excuses or plead extenuating circumstances.**

> As the Psalmist reminds us (David in his sin against Bathsheba and Uriah) yet ultimately:
>
> *[4]Against you, you only, have I sinned and done what is evil in your sight, so that you are proved right when you speak and justified when you judge.*
>
> Psalm 51:4.

* * * * *

CHAPTER 5

LIFE UNDER THE NEW MAN

5.1 INTRODUCTION

The possibility of living a life satisfying to God is premised on the fact that the Old Man is dead. He is dead "never to rise again".

Having sinned in Adam, we are reluctant to admit our position, because of the requirement to acknowledge and confess our sin and to return in repentance to God.

Jesus said to the Jews:

> [39]*You diligently study the Scriptures because you think that by them you possess eternal life. These are the Scriptures that testify about me,*
> [40]*yet **you refuse to come to me to have life**.*
>
> John 5:39-40, emphasis added.

Having *become sinners* by the **operation of the will**, we need to now *become Christians*—to have life—by the **operation of the will**. We need to consent to the mastery of Christ. We submit in unreserved trust (the fundamental characteristic of being human—as noted) to Christ as our Lord and Saviour.

And then we must continue in that consenting trust relationship:

> *⁶So then, just as you received Christ Jesus as Lord* [by faith], **continue** *to live in him* [by faith],
> *⁷rooted and built up in him, strengthened* **in the faith** *as you were taught ...*
>
> Colossians 2:6, emphases added.

And these continuing choices are made difficult by the years of living in the non-Christian state operating by the consent of the will to Satan and sin, and in particular, sinning by habits of the will. This is the legacy of the Old Man condition. And we shall note that these continuing choices are made by a *consenting* will, NOT an *achieving* will.

Hence, if like Paul we attempt to try to will good into operation, then like him, we shall fail:

> *¹⁵I do not understand what I do. For* **what I want to do I do not do, but what I hate I do.**
> *¹⁹For* **what I do is not the good I want to do; no, the evil I do not want to do—this I keep on doing**.
>
> Romans 7:15, 19, emphases added.

Resorting to his own will he is continually frustrated:

> *¹⁷For the sinful nature* (sic) [flesh] *desires what is contrary to the Spirit, and the Spirit what is contrary to the sinful nature* (sic) [flesh]. *They are in conflict with each other,* **so that you do not do what you want.**
>
> Galatians 5:17, emphasis added.

We noted in the early definition of sin, that *whatever is not of faith is sin*. Now there needs to be the operation of **faith** positively toward God, in all the decisions of life. The response to God is premised on the **operation of the will**.

The best loved verse of the Bible reminds us of this:

> *¹⁶"For God so loved the world that he gave his one and only Son, that* **whoever believes in him** *shall not perish but have eternal life* (John 3:16, emphasis added).

Having believed in Him, we are now in the New Man condition. The old has passed and the new has come. See earlier the treatment of 2 Corinthians 5:17.

5.2 MASTERY OF SIN REMOVED

Although the Christian has an ongoing struggle with temptation, and has many areas to be addressed, he is not under compulsion or mastery.

> ^{6}*For we know that our old self was crucified with him so that the body of sin might be done away with,* ***that we should no longer be slaves to sin****—*
> ^{7}*because anyone who has died has been **freed from sin**.*
>
> Romans 6:6, 7, emphasis added.

> ^{14} ... ***sin shall not be your master***
>
> Romans 6:14, emphasis added.

Even when we were in the non-Christian position, and ostensibly under the "mastery" of sin, we were still free to make a choice. Our wills are not entities that are powerless. We always are able to choose, even if we may have developed associations and habits that made the exercise of that choice very difficult.

Note again, as we reflect back on the Old Man condition, any mastery is subject to our wills, but THE problem revolves around the **habitual areas**. In the non-Christian condition it was natural to sin, and with a seared conscience, it was not difficult to continue in that direction without compunction. We filled out to the full the "works of the flesh"—none of them in themselves evil, but taken to excess or illicitly, they ensnare us in all our ways.

The problem now, is that we can still yield our wills to the pursuit of normal and natural appetites—but to excess—making them the "lusts" of the flesh, and resulting in a tacit submission to the mastery of Satan, who no longer has any claim on us.

Theoretically, we should have lost any appetite for sin. Should we go on sinning, doing evil under the guise of promoting grace?

> ²*By no means!* **We died to sin; how can we live in it any longer?**
> ¹⁸*You have been set free from sin and have become slaves to righteousness.*
>
> Romans 6:2, 18, emphasis added.

The tables have turned. No longer is sin our master, but we must master it. As God said to Cain:

> ⁷*If you do what is right, will you not be accepted? But if you do not do what is right,* **sin is crouching at your door; it desires to have you, but you must rule over** [master] *it."*
>
> Genesis 4:7, emphasis added.

5.3 FREEDOM NOT TO SIN
THE CONSENTING WILL

At no stage in the Christian experience is the will negated. Therefore, there is the possibility of sin. Hence we must be on the alert. And we must make choices in the context of the new life. It would still be possible to obey the dictates of the old experience, as we have just noted.

> ¹¹*In the same way, count yourselves* **dead to sin but alive to God** *in Christ Jesus.*
> ¹²*Therefore* **do not let sin reign** *in your mortal body so that you obey its evil desires.*
> ¹³**Do not offer the parts of your body to sin**, *as instruments of wickedness, but rather* **offer yourselves to God**, *as those who have been brought from death to life; and* **offer the parts** *of your body* **to him** *as instruments of righteousness.*
> ¹⁴*For* **sin shall not be your master**, *because you are not under law, but under grace.*
>
> Romans 6:11-14, emphases added.

It is a choice. It is our responsibility, therefore: ***do not** let sin reign in your mortal body* (verse 12), ***Do not** offer the parts of your body to sin* (verse 13). There is no longer any obligation to sin, we are under a new master. But we are not inert either, we have to make the choice, "DO NOT ...". It won't be automatic or enacted by a third party. And equally the Holy Spirit will not dictate our actions or force our hand.

Imagine a slave who has been sold to another master. He has been so used to serving the former that he struggles to adapt to the latter. And should he meet the former master, it would be very easy for him to succumb to any pressure the former master may seek to exert to obligate the slave to still obey him. If the former master were unscrupulous, he may play upon this deep-seated loyalty.

So it is with our status. We were slaves to sin under the mastery of Satan. But our Old Man is dead—finished in a completed act in the past. Our former master no longer has mastery over us (we are dead to sin), but it would be easy for us to yield out of **habit**. And if the former master—Satan—has no scruples—and he doesn't—he would try to keep us in subjection and fear of him.

So make the choice:

> [13]***Do not offer*** [go on offering—continuous] *the parts of your body **to sin**, as instruments of wickedness, but rather **offer** [go on offering—continuous] yourselves **to God**, as those who have been brought from death to life; and **offer** [go on offering—continuous] the parts of your body **to him** as instruments of righteousness.*
> [14]*For sin shall not be your master, because you are not under law, but under grace.*
>
> Romans 6:13, 14, emphases added.
>
> [16]*Don't you know that **when you offer** [continually] **yourselves to someone to obey** him as slaves, **you are slaves to the one***

whom you obey—*whether you are slaves to sin, which leads to death, or to obedience, which leads to righteousness?*
*¹⁷But thanks be to God that, though **you used to be slaves to sin**, you wholeheartedly obeyed the form of teaching to which you were entrusted.*
*¹⁸You have been **set free from sin and have become slaves to righteousness**.*
*¹⁹I put this in human terms because you are weak in your natural selves. Just as **you used to offer** the parts of your body in slavery to impurity and to ever-increasing wickedness, so **now offer** them in slavery to righteousness leading to holiness.*
²⁰When you were slaves to sin, you were free from the control of righteousness.
²¹What benefit did you reap at that time from the things you are now ashamed of? Those things result in death!
²²But now that you have been set free from sin and have become slaves to God, the benefit you reap leads to holiness, and the result is eternal life.
²³For the wages of sin is death, but the gift of God is eternal life in Christ Jesus our Lord.

Romans 6:16-23, emphases added.

At every point Paul emphasises the absolute requirement of choice—**the consenting will**.

Hence Paul addresses the issue of freedom and says to the Galatians:

¹³You, my brothers, were called to be free. But do not use your freedom to indulge the sinful nature (sic) [flesh] *rather, serve one another in love.*

Galatians 5:13.

You are free: **not to sin.** Your choice.

At times we may almost give up in despair, believing that the struggle is too hard and too continuous. But that freedom not to sin remains. Paul reminds us that there never is an impossible situation:

¹³No temptation has seized you except what is common to man. And God is faithful; **he will not let you be tempted beyond what you can bear.** *But when you are tempted, he will* **also provide a way out so that you can stand up under it.**

1 Corinthians 10:13, emphases added.

Our excuses are uncovered. If we succumb to sin, it is not because it was too hard, or because there was no way of escape; because God has stated emphatically that He will not allow us to be tempted beyond our capacity to endure.

And since we are not perfect, there will be sins, but they will be dealt with *en route* in the Christian experience. We note the relevance of 1 John 1:7, 9, which will be addressed in #5.5. HOW TO DEAL WITH SIN.

**NOTE: the consenting will operates not only in regard to whether or not we will sin, but also in regard to dealing with the already ingrained habits—the inculcated practices. Hence when dealing with these practices, which we are inadequate to address completely—hence Paul's despair of Romans Chapter 7—we need to consent to the Holy Spirit Who can help. We look at this in the next section.

5.4 LIFE UNDER GRACE

In the new life in Christ, although we are under grace, we are not given licence to sin. As we noted, we are "free NOT to sin". It is a choice.

The self-love of the Old Man condition is now changed by the Spirit-directed ego of the New Man.

However, we have a responsibility to respond to God by faith in "repatterning" our behaviour. There has been a fundamental change of our being in putting off the Old Man and then putting on the New Man. Those old habits and practices ingrained in the Old Man condition, must now be deliberately replaced by the habits and practices of the New Man. And this won't just happen by chance or incidentally. The process of "repatternization" will only occur by strong and deliberate determination—the will.

BUT, this is not an *achieving* will, it is a *consenting* will. When we consent to Christ in salvation, we do not achieve anything of ourselves, it is the gift of God:

> [8]*For it is by grace you have been saved, through faith—and this **not from yourselves**, it is the gift of God—*
> [9]***not by works**, so that no one can boast.*
>
> Ephesians 2:8, 9, emphases added.

Likewise, in our Christian walk, we do not *achieve* anything of ourselves. We cannot "will" jealousy away by our own efforts, or "will" the good, something that Paul discovered he so miserably failed in, as we have noted in Romans 7:15-20. And yet there is clear expectation for us to deal with the old habits.

****NOTE:** the area of real difficulty is the HABIT area—see below.

And note that the following instructions to deal with the ingrained habits, are all given by Paul in the context of the Old Man/New Man discussion, in the **three** passages already noted.

5.4.1 ROMANS 6 (and following).

Grace gives us liberty, but not licence:

> [15]*What then? Shall we sin because we are not under law but under grace? By no means!*
>
> Romans 6:15.

Grace is not freedom to sin, but freedom **not** to sin.

> [4]*So, my brothers, you also died to the law through the body of Christ, that you might belong to another, to him who was raised from the dead, in order that we might **bear fruit to God**.*

> *⁵For when we were controlled by the sinful nature* [sic], *the sinful passions aroused by the law were at work in our bodies, so that we bore fruit for death.*
> *⁶But* **now, by dying to what once bound us, we have been released from the law so that we serve in the new way of the Spirit,** *and not in the old way of the written code.*
>
> Romans 7:4-6, emphases added.

We are now living in the New Man condition, under the mastery of the Holy Spirit: **we serve in the new way of the Spirit**—the life under grace.

We have already seen this principle of the new way of the Spirit, in the study of Galatians 5, when looking at the flesh.

> ¹⁶*So I say,* **live by the Spirit***, and you will not gratify the desires of the sinful nature* (sic) [flesh – sarx].
>
> Galatians 5:16, emphasis added.

This is the way of the New Man, and if followed, it will dramatically affect our behaviour.

- "gratify" = fulfil *teleō* (τελεω): means to give effect to, to complete or perfect, to bring to an end, bring to a conclusion, to carry out to the full. There is no attempt to deny the normal desires of the flesh, but like all temptation, it does not have to find extreme fulfilment. We do not have to consummate **the lust** of the flesh—we are not under compulsion. There is no bypassing of our wills. But under the constraint of the Spirit, and with our consent—to live by the Spirit—we will not indulge the flesh. We will not consummate the passions to an extreme that is sinful.

We belong to Christ, and we entered that through the death of the Old Man AND the death of the passions—the extremes—of the flesh. See earlier under Chapter 2, #C. THE FLESH.

> ²⁴*Those who belong to Christ Jesus have crucified the sinful nature* (sic) *with its passions and desires* (Galatians 5:24).

**NOTE: flesh, *sarx*. NOT NATURE. Of itself the desires of the flesh are normal and natural, but it is the passions and desires taken to extreme that cause the problem.

And let it be stated again (and again), that the fulfilment of the natural desires, is by the operation of the will, and then there is a continuum through to the area where these natural fulfilments are out of control, so we must act decisively to counter this:

> *¹²Therefore **do not let sin reign** in your mortal body so that you obey its evil desires.*
> *¹³**Do not offer** the parts of your body to sin, as instruments of wickedness, but rather **offer yourselves to God**, as those who have been brought from death to life; and offer the parts of your body to him as instruments of righteousness.*
>
> Romans 6:12, 13, emphases added.

- *Do not let sin reign:* **note:** this is **a choice**. Operation of the will. And it is the negation of continuity—not of perfection.
- *Do not offer:* **note:** this is **a choice**.
- *Offer yourselves:* a positive **choice**.

Part of the life under grace is the development of clear choices based on identifying issues that must be addressed and "put off" or resisted, together with making positive choices of identified areas that are honouring to God.

There is another very significant factor that must be emphasised shortly; **mortification of the practices** through a consenting will to the Holy Spirit

5.4.2 EPHESIANS 4 (and following).

Further, in this second passage relating to the Old Man, there are positive choices that are enjoined, as well as choices to avoid negative influences.

[14] ... ***clothe yourselves*** *with the Lord Jesus Christ, and **do not think** about how to gratify the desires of the sinful nature* (sic) [flesh].

Ephesians 4:14, emphases added.

Here there are both positive as well as negative instructions. By positively recognising your position in Christ, this will help to redirect your attention away from the flesh—NOT the flesh as if that were intrinsically sinful—but away from the **sinful desires** of the flesh. It may seem a little pedantic and nit-picking, but it is nevertheless very important to keep the right balance. Remember, there is nothing wrong with the basic natural desires of the flesh. Food is fine, sex is fine, etc.—in their right balance. It is pursuing these desires to an UN-natural level that is the problem. And because of our **habitual** behaviour in the Old Man condition, we have this "repatternization" problem that can be a block in the life under grace, as we are re-learning.

Paul addresses many of these attitudinal things:

[23] ... *be made **new in the attitude of your minds**;*
[24] and to put on the new self (sic) [man], *created to be like God in true righteousness and holiness.*
*[25] Therefore each of you **must put off falsehood and speak truthfully** to his neighbour, for we are all members of one body.*
*[26] "**In your anger do not sin**": Do not let the sun go down while you are still angry,*
*[27] and **do not give the devil a foothold**.*
*[28] He who has been stealing must **steal no longer**, but must **work, doing something useful** with his own hands, that he may have something to share with those in need.*
*[29] **Do not let any unwholesome talk come out of your mouths**, but **only what is helpful** for building others up according to their needs, that it may benefit those who listen.*
*[30] And **do not grieve the Holy Spirit of God**, with whom you were sealed for the day of redemption.*
*[31] **Get rid of all bitterness, rage and anger, brawling and slander, along with every form of malice.***

*³²**Be kind and compassionate** to one another, **forgiving each other**, just as in Christ God forgave you.*
*¹**Be imitators of God**, therefore, as dearly loved children*
*²and **live a life of love**, just as Christ loved us and gave himself up for us as a fragrant offering and sacrifice to God.*
³But among you there must not be even a hint of sexual immorality, or of any kind of impurity, or of greed, because these are improper for God's holy people.
⁴Nor should there be obscenity, foolish talk or coarse joking, which are out of place, but rather thanksgiving.

Ephesians 4:23-5:4, emphases added.

These injunctions are mostly straightforward, but just a note:

- ***In your anger do not sin*** (verse 26): even "righteous indignation" must be tempered. "Anger": *orgizō* (ὀργιζω): originally any "natural impulse, or desire, or disposition," came to signify "anger," as the strongest of all passions. It is to be distinguished from *thumos* (wrath—not translated as "anger"): "in this respect, that *thumos* indicates a more agitated condition of the feelings, an outburst of wrath from inward indignation, while *orgē* suggests a more settled or abiding condition of mind, frequently with a view to taking revenge. *Orgē* is less sudden in its rise than *thumos*, but more lasting in its nature. *Thumos* expresses more the inward feeling, *orgē* the more active emotion. *Thumos* may issue in revenge, though it does not necessarily include it. It is characteristic that it quickly blazes up and quickly subsides, though that is not necessarily implied in each case (Vine, *et al*, 1996, Vol. 2, 26).

**NOTE: there is an appropriate place for "anger"—which is a settled position. God has a settled position with regard to sin. He is "angry" (a settled position) with the wicked every day (Psalm 7:11, A.V.). But if we allow this anger to become vindictive or to seek vengeance, then there is a problem.

5.4.3 COLOSSIANS 3 (and following).

In the third passage addressing the Old Man, the instructions are similar—and again they are all premised upon choices—the operation of the will. Both positive as well as negative.

> [5]***Put to death***, *therefore, whatever belongs to your earthly nature* (sic) [members]: ***sexual immorality, impurity, lust, evil desires and greed, which is idolatry***.
> [7]*You used to walk in these ways, in the life you once lived.*
> [8]*But now you must **rid yourselves** of all such things as these: **anger, rage, malice, slander, and filthy language from your lips**.*
> [9]***Do not lie*** *to each other, since you have taken off your old self* (sic)[man] *with its practices*
> [10]*and have put on the new self* (sic) [man], *which is being renewed ...*
> [12]*Therefore, as God's chosen people, holy and dearly loved,* ***clothe yourselves with compassion, kindness, humility, gentleness and patience***.
> [13]***Bear with each other*** *and **forgive** whatever grievances you may have against one another. Forgive as the Lord forgave you*

Colossians 3:5, 7-10, 12-13, emphases added.

- "put to death" (verse 5): *nekrōsate* (νεκρωσατε), "to put to death," is used in the active voice in the sense of destroying the strength of, depriving of power, with reference to the evil desires which work in the body (Vine, *et al*, 1996, Vol. 2, 148). The inherent power of the Old Man ingrained in the body (the limbs) must be deactivated.

- "(earthly) nature" (verse 5): *melē* (μελη), "limbs of the body" (Vine, *et al*, 1996, Vol. 2, 402). The phrase is literally: "**limbs** upon the earth". "Earthly nature" is a seriously misleading translation. These are the limbs, as opposed to the trunk, that must now be addressed. The trunk, as it were, the Old Man, has been crucified, now it is the aspects of this body that must be addressed.

**NOTE: This word, *melē*, limb, is used in the context of the human body and also compared to the body—the church—in Romans 12:4, 5, emphases added:

> *⁴Just as each of us has **one body with many members** (melē), and these **members** (melē) do **not all have the same function** (praxis = practice),*
> *⁵so in Christ we who are **many form one body**, and **each member** (melē) **belongs** to all the others.*

NOTE: the serious diversity of terms that are nevertheless translated with the one term "nature**", thus confusing the whole issue. The Old Man is "translated" as the "old **nature**". The "flesh" is translated as "old **nature**". The "limbs" (of the earth) are translated as (earthly) "**nature**". If the translations were accurate, there would be far less confusion.

- "you have taken off your old self [man] with its practices" (verse 9): hence there is now no obligation to continue these habits. Especially now that you have "put on the new man". You have been "married to another" (Romans 7:3-4), so serve the new partner. The Old Man is dead, so he is no problem, but it is the ingrained habits in the body that need to be "repatterned".

- "is being renewed" (verse 10): *anakainoō* (ἀνακαινοω), "to make new" (*ana*, "back" or "again," *kainos*, "new," not recent but different), "to renew," (Vine, *et al*, 1996, Vol. 2, 524). The verb is a present passive participle, indicating the ongoing work associated with having put on the New Man. We are becoming different. This is the process of sanctification.

NOTE: as a matter of interest: in this verse, New Man is *veos,* and *the process* is *ana*kainoō***, (kainos)* whereas the passage in Ephesians 4:23, 24, *the process* of being renewed is *ananeoomai (neos),* and the New Man is ***kainos***. See further on the contrast in #3.3.2. THE NEW MAN.

5.4.4 MORTIFYING THE HABITS/PRACTICES.

In the three passages, it is very clear that we are commanded to:

1) In **Romans 6**, make choices about who we are now to obey (Romans 6:12, 13, 16).

2) In **Ephesians 4**, we are to put off the evils of the old life, and to clothe ourselves with (put on) Christ, adopting new attitudes.

3) In **Colossians 3** we are to put to death the practices of the old life and to clothe ourselves with positive behaviours.

The question now becomes, **"How do we achieve this?"**

We have already noted that our wills are not *achieving* wills, but *consenting* wills.

The most helpful instructions come from Romans 7, especially in the section where Paul laments his abysmal failure to adequately deal with the practices of his Christian experience (verses 7-8). It is this area of practices/habits that is THE problem that we are addressing in this book. We will look at this in more detail in the next section as we examine the whole issue of DEALING WITH SIN, especially #5.5.1 3), HABIT SIN.

5.5 HOW TO DEAL WITH SIN—
IN THE THREE CATEGORIES OF SIN
(Introduced in #4.2).

5.5.1 INTRODUCTION: COMMON GROUND

As we look at this whole issue of dealing with sin (deliberate, unintentional, habit), although there are very different situations with the three categories, nevertheless there is some common ground and basic principles.

1) THE WILL—the operation of the consenting will.

Fundamental to our understanding of sin, is the involvement of the **will**. In #2.2 we looked at the matter of THE MOTIVATION FOR SIN: THE OPERATION OF THE WILL. Our will is not corrupted. Our will is not rendered ineffective. The will in fact is inert. (See the correctives above, as well as in *Condemned Already*, Swincer 2011a).

There are factors that may affect our decision making. There are many influences. There are desires of the flesh. But ultimately we must make the choice.

In #4.2 we addressed the THREE CATEGORIES OF SIN, and in that section we noted that the will is primarily a direct problem with Deliberate Sin, but it is also indirectly involved in Habit Sin, so let us look at some principles for the operation of the will.

We have made an application to the matter of **food** in several places already. But now, to look at the matter of the will in dealing with the potential for sin, and how to seek a corrective.

Reminder—food is fine, and a healthy appetite is perfectly OK. It is on the occasions when this normal gets out of control that there is a problem—and this starts to enter the habit area. If we want to deal with the potential for sin, we may have to adjust behaviour so that we do not sin.

If I have a problem with overindulging in food, I need to learn to push my chair back from the table, when I could still go on eating but don't need to. Everyone else is still eating ravenously, there is still plenty of beautiful food on the table, and my mouth is still watering. But I must take control—there is no other "nature" or third party to do it.

This may be the **first step: prohibition/preclusion**. I actually push back and remove myself from the temptation. I am "prevented"—by choice—from participation.

This step must only ever be temporary. We do not learn self-discipline by exclusion. Putting the cake tin on the top shelf does not teach a child discipline. He has no option. There is a physical prohibition.

The **next steps** may be **graded access.** At a meal (potluck dinner!?) I can stay sitting within easy reach of the food, preferably not immediately at the table, and instead of having to push away from the table, I learn to sit within easy access and simply say "no" to myself. I may need to be able to resist the coercion of a generous host exhorting me to "have some more". It is my choice.

Part of this graded access might be that I then learn to sit back at the table right up against the food, but select only sufficient as I need.

This process might well be assisted by a third party to help with accountability. See below at 3). **ACCOUNT-ABILITY.**

Returning to the graded process.

My elder daughter was (is still) a self-confessed chocoholic. She could barely pass a store without wanting to buy some chocolate—and there would be nothing left from the last purchase!! There was this "compulsion", that probably fits more into the area of habit sins, but nevertheless, she realised it was getting *out* of control and she needed to *take* control. One of the strategies I suggested to her, was that she get some chocolate, sit down at her desk to do her study, and put some of the chocolate at the other end of the desk out of reach—interim "prohibition". She could still see it, even smell it, but she was to leave it for a given time period of say 15 minutes. Subsequently, she would repeat the exercise, but leave the chocolate for 30 minutes. And then grade through to the stage where she put the chocolate right beside her at her desk, and yet leave it for a set period of time.

Because of sharing with me, there was the additional help of "accountability". I could enquire about her progress or otherwise. And this "pressure" of accountability was helpful.

By working through incremental stages, with achievable goals, she could regain control of this "normal" appetite.

True victory only comes when this denial can be done under extreme circumstances—leave the chocolate right beside her for, say, 2 hours.

We spoke previously of someone being ravenous for food, in #2.3 THE FLESH, and how even with a ravenous appetite, the intervention of fire would easily transcend that appetite in order to save life. Such a seemingly extreme hunger could in fact be delayed for several hours.

We don't necessarily have to put ourselves through extremes, but occasionally that might be necessary to prove a point. And we can't even start to imagine what such an extreme might be in the normal run of events, but we can be helped by remembering that Jesus has been there. We noted in passing that Jesus was tempted—purely from the perspective of temptation. But **we now note the extremity. He fasted for 40 days and 40 nights,** and the Gospel of Matthew comments rather benignly: *After fasting forty days and forty nights, he was hungry* (Matthew 4:2). Hungry indeed! That has to be a remarkable understatement! I barely fast between meals—but to fast for 40 days! Suffice it to say, that we can seek Jesus' help for "dealing with sin"—in this case gluttony, from the perspective of the operation of the will to control that normal appetite.

If we can push back from the table after sitting there for 40 days without eating anything, I think we have the problem licked! (pun intended). That is when we can claim a **victory** in that area of discipline.

Jesus understands, because He has been to the extremity in His fasting, and He did not give in:

*¹⁵For we do not have a high priest who is unable to sympathize with our weaknesses, but we have one who has been **tempted in every way, just as we are—yet was without sin**.*

Hebrews 4:15, emphasis added.

Consequently, we can unashamedly seek His help:

*¹⁶Let us then approach the throne of grace **with confidence**, so that **we may receive mercy and find grace to help** us in our time of need.*

Hebrews 4:16, emphases added.

Although the issues are different for a recovering **alcoholic**—due to addiction as well as failure to operate with the will—nevertheless the principles are similar. Ultimately it is the operation of the will that will lead to full recovery.

The **first step** would no doubt be **prohibition/preclusion**. The alcoholic would not be helped by fraternising with drinkers or visiting shops or bars where alcohol might be readily available.

The **next steps** would be **graded accessibility**, but denying participation. He must be able to make choices about alcohol—and he won't learn that through preclusion alone.

No doubt he would be assisted through the graded process by the support of others in **accountability**, whether through an AA program or personal friends, or both.

Ultimately, there could be the stage when he can actually hold a glass of his favourite alcoholic beverage in his hand, smell it, look at it, and then pour it down the drain without any regret.

At that stage he will be well on the way to **victory** over that addiction.

Apply the will with determination—but be reasonable in practical application.

**NOTE: about victory:

Beware of assuming that a victory is ever permanent. The biggest danger is to think that we have succeeded in finally defeating a problem. Heed the Word of God:

> *¹²So, **if you think you are standing firm, be careful that you don't fall!***
>
> 1 Corinthians 10:12, emphasis added.

Always be on guard, but avoid being paranoid.

2) ATTITUDE OF THE MIND.

In passing we have noticed the imperative:

> *²³ ... be made new in the **attitude of your minds**;*
>
> Ephesians 4:23, emphasis added.

This aspect cannot be emphasized too much. **All** sin is related to the **mind** (except the unintentional sins—and they are minimal in most experience), as was noted in the definitions of sin. It is from the mind that there is rebellion, and lack of faith or persuasion, and all that results from responding to temptation.

Like the **will**, the **mind** is fundamental to the whole issue of now dealing with sin. Again, we recall that in #4.2, in looking at the THREE CATEGORIES OF SIN, that the mind was significant especially in the area of Deliberate Sin, but also was relevant to Habit Sin.

There are principles here that are helpful for the whole of our spiritual walk, and therefore also helpful in the whole area of decision-making—the operation of the consenting will.

At the very foundation, we have to admit our true condition. God says (Jeremiah 17:9, NKJV, emphasis added):

> *⁹ "**The heart is deceitful above all things**,*
> *And desperately wicked;*
> *Who can know it?*

When Jesus was sharing the Last Supper with His disciples, He declared to them, that one of them would betray Him. Almost innocently, the very betrayer on the verge of carrying out that pernicious act, asks Jesus: *"Surely not I, Rabbi?"* (Matthew 26:25). How deceitful is the heart!

But Peter is equally oblivious to his true ability to handle his situation.

> *³¹Then Jesus told them, "This very night **you will all fall away on account of me** ...*
> *³³**Peter replied**, "Even if all fall away on account of you, **I never will**."*
> *³⁴"I tell you the truth," Jesus answered, "this very night, before the rooster crows, you will disown me three times."*
> *³⁵But Peter declared, "**Even if I have to die with you, I will never disown you**." And all the other disciples said the same.*
>
> Matthew 26:31-35, emphases added.

And we know the sad sequel. It is imperative to know our hearts, and to take all precautions to protect our integrity. The Bible warns, as we just noted above:

> *¹² ... **if you think you are standing firm, be careful that you don't fall!***
>
> 1 Corinthians 10:12, emphasis added.

We have looked at **five pivotal issues** in our understanding of the issue of the Christian and his culpability for his sin. But as far as **dealing with sin** is concerned, in addition to these pivotal areas, there is—**ONE CRUCIAL ISSUE: THE MIND (the heart).**

Nothing is more fundamental than the involvement of the **mind**. Even if we take note of nothing else in this study, but give careful attention to the **mind**, we will probably succeed in dealing with sin!

It is the mind (or heart) that is the source of habitual sin. It is the preoccupation with thoughts that lead to lust and

imagination that leads to strategies and the resultant sinful behaviour.

But a habit can also be as innocuous as the alarm in the morning. Switch it off often enough and just roll over and go back to sleep, and before long you won't even hear it. There is a conditioned response as part of the habit that you are forming.

Or if you live near a railway track, or an airport, the frequent passing of trains or aircraft results in a conditioned response and you don't even hear them. When a visitor comes to supper they might suddenly exclaim, "How do you put up with that noise?" And you blithely reply, "What noise?" You have developed a conditioned response, which is a habit, and you don't hear the train or aircraft. In this case it is probably good to have developed that response, but that is not applicable to all situations.

It is easy to delude ourselves about whether or not we can handle temptation, or resist the desire to pursue old habits that we think are now under control. We might **think** that we can handle it. We need to acknowledge that God knows all about us, and in particular:

> [10] *"I the LORD* **search the heart** *and* **examine the mind**, *to reward a man according to his conduct, according to what his deeds deserve."*

Jeremiah 17:10, emphases added.

That being the case, let us openly request that the Lord does that precisely for us personally in the variety of situations that are presented to us. We need to pray with the Psalmist:

> [23]***Search me, O God, and know my heart; test me and know my anxious thoughts.***
> [24]*See if there is any offensive way in me, and lead me in the way everlasting.*

Psalm 139:23, 24, emphases added.

Likewise the writer of the Proverbs urges:

*²³**Keep your heart with all diligence,*
*For **out of it spring the issues of life.***

Proverbs 4:23 (NKJV), emphases added.

And he continues to advise other ways to help to keep free from sin:

*²**Put away **from you a deceitful mouth,*
And put perverse lips far from you.
*²⁵**Let your eyes look straight ahead,*
And your eyelids look right before you.
²⁶Ponder the path of your feet,
*And **let all your ways be established.***
²⁷Do not turn to the right or the left;
Remove your foot from evil.

Proverbs 4:24-27 (NKJV), emphases added.

These are areas which will affect our thinking—areas where we are needing to make decisions, and we need to respond in a way that is appropriate and constructive—in **speaking, looking, walking**.

But at the root of it, we need to know our **hearts (our minds—what we are thinking).** As Proverbs reminds us:

⁷For as [a man] ***thinks in his heart**, so is he ...*

Proverbs 23:7, emphasis added.

What we think—whatever preoccupies our minds—becomes translated into actions and eventually typifies us.

We noted earlier the importance of what we **think**, in referring to Jesus' words in the context of habit sins, that the mouth expresses the spontaneous overflow of the **heart**. But the principle is also foundational for the whole of life's attitudes:

*³⁴You brood of vipers, how can you who are evil say anything good? For **out of the overflow of the heart the mouth speaks**.*

*[35]The **good man** brings **good things** out of the **good stored** up in him, and the **evil man** brings **evil things** out of the **evil stored** up in him.*

Matthew 12:34-35, emphases added.

Jesus goes further to explain to the disciples how important it is to recognise the **heart** (mind) as the source of good or evil, and it is not related to external washing or otherwise:

*[11]**What goes into a man's mouth does not make him 'unclean,' but what comes out of his mouth, that is what makes him 'unclean.'***

[17]"Don't you see that whatever enters the mouth goes into the stomach and then out of the body?

[18]But the things that come out of the mouth come from the heart, and these make a man 'unclean.'

*[19]For **out of the heart come evil thoughts, murder, adultery, sexual immorality, theft, false testimony, slander**.*

[20]These are what make a man 'unclean';

Matthew 15:11, 17-20, emphases added.

In addition to what Jesus is warning about the overflow of a man's heart via his mouth, is the way the mouth speaks that is also a matter of concern. We can speak caustically, lovingly, roughly, kindly, etc. And this in itself can be sinful. Let us pray with the Psalmist:

[3]Set a guard over my mouth, O LORD; keep watch over the door of my lips.

Psalm 141:3.

Adding to the reference by Jesus with regard to the heart or mind affecting the words of a man, noted in Matthew, Paul (likewise) suggests very strongly—in the book of Romans—that we need a renewal of the **mind** in order to not conform to the *patterns* of the world. By contrast, we need to be "repatterned" in the matter of **attitudes** to avoid the habit sins that are already "patterned" in us (see below).

> ²*Do not conform any longer to the pattern of this world, but be transformed by the renewing of your mind. Then you will be able to test and approve what God's will is—his good, pleasing and perfect will.*
>
> Romans 12:2, emphases added.

Our deliberate choices must be free of "patterned" responses. When we can think clearly about the things of God with a right attitude, then this is the basis of correct decisions.

As a young man of about 17 years of age, I was acutely aware of this need to keep a right attitude, and the following Psalm was a great personal challenge to me:

> ⁹*How can a young man keep his way pure?* ***By living according to your word.***
> ¹⁰***I seek you with all my heart****; do not let me stray from your commands.*
> ¹¹***I have hidden your word in my heart THAT I MIGHT NOT SIN AGAINST YOU.***
>
> Psalm 119:9-11, emphases added.

It is this area of an **effective devotional life** that is the greatest antidote to sin of all categories.

The devotional life is imperative. Don't complain about problems with dealing with sin if your devotional life is not effective. Work on that area as a priority.

Subsequently, my personal Bible memorization program was reinvigorated—God's Word hidden in my **heart**. I wanted to do everything within my power to make sure that my **mind** was set on the things of God.

I wanted to make sure that "the good stored up" in me, was God's Word. I wanted the "overflow" of my casual conversation, as well as the unexpected exclamations in extremities, to be well-pleasing to God.

Paul reinforces this idea to the Philippians:

> *⁸Finally, brothers, whatever is **true**, whatever is **noble**, whatever is **right**, whatever is **pure**, whatever is **lovely**, whatever is **admirable**—if anything is excellent or praiseworthy—**THINK about such things**.*
>
> Philippians 4:8, emphases added.

It is our choice to feed our **minds** on helpful and productive matters. To study the Word of God. To hide God's Word in our hearts.

This basic information will help us in making **deliberate** choices so that we do not sin. It will help us to have a basis of helpful attitudes to **practice** in place of the old habits—and Paul precisely continues in that context (of Philippians):

> *⁹Whatever you have learned or received or heard from me, or seen in me—**put it into practice** [a new **habit**].*
>
> Philippians 4:9, emphasis added.

This preparation of heart and mind in regard to biblical and positive things helps us to be **alert** and **aware** of the enemy and this is especially applicable as a preparation to avoid **unwitting sins**—see below—as well as being a basis for correct decisions as a corrective against **deliberate sins**.

After more than fifty years of ministry and counselling, I have never come across a case where a man has awakened one morning, thrown back the bed clothes, walked across to the window, thrown open the curtains, opened the windows, looked out on the new day, and declared, "I think I will go and commit adultery today!" Never.

It all starts in the **mind**. There is an inadvertent and/or compromising situation—quite unexpected. And if the devotional life is not currently effective, the person is taken off guard. There is a flutter of the heart, and the mind starts to play the event over and over. Soon there are subtle ideas of how the situation might be replicated. Plans develop in order to execute those ideas.

Another "accidental" encounter might be orchestrated, and a "testing of the waters". Did the other party have any interest? Was the initial event with or without intent?

The behaviour may have to be modified, but the plans will go on. The **mind** is preoccupied with ideas and strategies. And so the fool goes headlong, obsessed with his goal, and will not rest until he has achieved his goal, only to find that he has sacrificed all for a moment of base pleasure:

> ^{22}*All at once he followed her like an ox going to the slaughter, like a deer stepping into a noose*
> ^{23}*till* **an arrow pierces his liver***, like* **a bird darting into a snare, little knowing it will cost him his life***.*
>
> Proverbs 7:22-23, emphases added.

Too late he realises he is trapped. He is caught, and it may "cost him his life".

The wisdom of the Proverbs is a great help for these practicalities of life. Read it chapter by chapter regularly.

a) SLIPPERY DIP TO HELL.

The first look cannot be avoided. It is unexpected.

It is what happens next that may destroy your life.

1) A second, and/or third, etc. **deliberate** look—it is a choice with a consenting will—a long and lusting look that sets the heart racing, and raises the potential for a slippery dip to destruction. Plans are soon in motion. **OR,**

2) You immediately make reference of your life to God:

    - "Lord, guide my eyes, You saw what I saw, help me to look straight ahead" (Proverbs 4:25).

        And: "Turn my eyes away from worthless things ..." (Psalm 119:37)

- "Lord, examiner of the hearts of men, guide my thinking—search me and know my thoughts right now ... and lead me in Your ways".

The alternative you choose will indicate your true position before God.

Look carefully at the following two cases, to compare these two alternatives.

b) CASE STUDY: KING DAVID.

King David was such a one as the man about whom we have being reflecting. (The following verses from 2 Samuel 11).

> [1]*In the spring, **at the time when kings go off to war**, David sent Joab out with the king's men and the whole Israelite army. ... But **David remained in Jerusalem**.*

Right at the start, David was in the wrong place. Normally he would be leading the army at this "**time when kings go off to war**", but he remained in Jerusalem. And then the unexpected happened.

> [2]*One evening David got up from his bed and walked around on the roof of the palace. From the roof he saw a woman bathing. The woman was very beautiful,*

Instead of having some devotions and committing the situation to the Lord, David played out the whole scenario in his mind. And he liked it, and he wanted more—

> [3]*and David sent someone to find out about her.*

And so he started to plan and scheme, in spite of his information that she was a married woman:

> [3] *... The man said, "Isn't this Bathsheba, the daughter of Eliam and the wife of Uriah the Hittite?"*

There was no excuse for David now, but in the absence of any devotions, he pursued his selfish desires—even if fundamentally the sex drive is normal (and how many wives and concubines did he have?! See Nathan's parable below). He should have had this principle from the Proverbs in his mind as a corrective and deterrent:

> *²¹For a man's ways are **in full view of the LORD**, and he examines all his paths.*
>
> Proverbs 5:21, emphasis added.

But he didn't, so (resuming 2 Samuel 11):

> *⁴Then David sent messengers to get her. She came to him, and he slept with her ... Then she went back home.*
> *⁵The woman conceived and sent word to David, saying, "I am pregnant."*

David is caught. "*(a)n arrow pierces his liver*" (Proverbs 7:23). Having failed to use any contraceptive(!) he now has to try to cover his sin.

> *⁶So David sent this word to Joab* [the captain in his army]: *"Send me Uriah the Hittite."* [the woman's husband] *And Joab sent him to David.*
> *⁷When Uriah came to him, David asked him how Joab was, how the soldiers were and how the war was going.*
> *⁸Then David said to Uriah, "Go down to your house and wash your feet." So Uriah left the palace, and a gift from the king was sent after him.*

David sent for Uriah and brought him home from the battle. He thus compromises others—including his commander, Joab—and plans to let Uriah have some recreation leave, hoping that he might have sex with his wife in order to try to cover for her pregnancy. He seeks to ingratiate himself to Uriah, sending him a gift. BUT:

> *⁹But Uriah slept at the entrance to the palace with all his master's servants and did not go down to his house.*

David's plans fail. The sweaty "work of the flesh" is not beneficial. But he can't give up now. He drives ahead with modified plans. And he doesn't consult God.

> *¹⁰When David was told, "Uriah did not go home," he asked him, "Haven't you just come from a distance? Why didn't you go home?"*
> *¹¹Uriah said to David, "The ark and Israel and Judah are staying in tents, and my master Joab and my lord's men are camped in the open fields. How could I go to my house to eat and drink and lie with my wife? As surely as you live, I will not do such a thing!"*

David should have been rebuked by the honourable answer of Uriah. Nothing base even passed Uriah's mind. And yet here is a "man after God's own heart" (Acts 13:22) plunging headlong into more and more sin. It is not a matter of what David should have been. The fact is that he failed because he made no reference of his life to God in that situation. Past victories are no guarantee for success in future episodes. Each case must be treated on the same principles.

It was not as though David was unfamiliar with that principle of seeking God. Many a time in battle he had sought the Lord as his first reference point. For example:

> *¹⁸Now the Philistines had come and spread out in the Valley of Rephaim;*
> *¹⁹so David inquired of the LORD, "**Shall I go** and attack the Philistines? **Will you hand them over to me?**" The LORD answered him, "**Go, for I will surely hand the Philistines over to you.**"*
>
> 2 Samuel 5:18-19, emphases added.

So David went up to fight, and God gave him the victory. God's will was clear and specific. But the Philistines were not prepared to take defeat, and they again came up for battle, and again David enquired of the Lord:

> *²²Once more the Philistines came up and spread out in the Valley of Rephaim;*

> [23]*so **David inquired of the LORD**, and he answered, "**Do not go straight up,** but circle around behind them and attack them in front of the balsam trees.*
> [24]*As soon as you hear the sound of marching in the tops of the balsam trees, move quickly, because that will mean the LORD has gone out in front of you to strike the Philistine army."*
>
> 2 Samuel 5:22-24, emphases added.

This time the Lord not only approved the request, but also gave David the strategy for success. And these, and other examples, occurred *before* the episode with Bathsheba. He should have maintained his **practice**.

Returning to the story with Bathsheba, David was hell-bent on his corrupt plan. He was desperate to make it appear that Bathsheba had fallen pregnant to Uriah. Not only did he get him to remain longer in Jerusalem, but he entertained him and tried to get him drunk in order to manipulate him further:

> [12]*Then David said to him, "Stay here one more day, and tomorrow I will send you back." So Uriah remained in Jerusalem that day and the next.*
> [13]*At David's invitation, he ate and drank with him, and David made him drunk. But in the evening Uriah went out to sleep on his mat among his master's servants; he did not go home.*

Things were getting difficult. But the sweaty energy of the flesh drove David on. He now hatched a plan to compromise his general, Joab, by seeking to have Uriah in the heat of battle, hoping that he would be killed:

> [14]*In the morning David wrote a letter to Joab and sent it with Uriah.*
> [15]*In it he wrote, "Put Uriah in the front line where the fighting is fiercest. Then withdraw from him so he will be struck down and die."*

David is so desperate that he throws caution to the wind, and clearly states his intention. He wants an innocent man killed. Unwittingly (to a point) Joab obliges:

¹⁶So while Joab had the city under siege, he put Uriah at a place where he knew the strongest defenders were.
¹⁷When the men of the city came out and fought against Joab, some of the men in David's army fell; moreover, Uriah the Hittite died.

Joab fears that there may be some recriminations from the king for the conduct of the battle when he sends his full account to David, but he knows that he can easily placate him:

*²¹ ... If he asks you this (about the questionable battle strategy), then say to him, '**Also, your servant Uriah the Hittite is dead.**'*

And so a messenger reported to David about the battle, and in particular that Uriah was dead.

David has no remorse, and no awareness of his own escalating sin. When he receives the message, his casual reply to Joab is:

*²⁵David told the messenger, "Say this to Joab: '**Don't let this upset you**; the sword devours one as well as another. Press the attack against the city and destroy it.' Say this to encourage Joab."*

Uriah was quite expendable for David's selfish and sinful plan. He adds murder to adultery without compunction. Where is there any reference to God?

Bathsheba heard about her husband and she mourned for him, but there was no time lost after the official "time of mourning was over":

*²⁷After the time of mourning was over, David had her brought to his house, and she became his wife and bore him a son. But **the thing David had done displeased the LORD**.*

(The above selections from 2 Samuel 11, emphases added).

But still there was no evidence of shame or remorse at all. In our terms, David's devotional life was dead. God did not enter his considerations. And he deliberately sinned—and he alone was responsible. And it never occurred to him that he was out of line. God graciously brought a rebuke to David.

Whilst David thought that he could *cover* for his sins, God used the prophet Nathan to *expose* his sin, by confronting him with the truth about his actions. Using a parable, Nathan didn't waste time in getting to the point.

> [1] **The LORD sent Nathan to David.** *When he came to him, he said, "There were two men in a certain town, one rich and the other poor.*
> [2] *The rich man had a very large number of sheep and cattle,*
> [3] *but the poor man had nothing except one little ewe lamb he had bought. He raised it, and it grew up with him and his children. It shared his food, drank from his cup and even slept in his arms. It was like a daughter to him.*
> [4] *"Now a traveller came to the rich man, but the rich man refrained from taking one of his own sheep or cattle to prepare a meal for the traveller who had come to him. Instead, he took the ewe lamb that belonged to the poor man and prepared it for the one who had come to him."*

2 Samuel 12:1-4, emphasis added.

The expected response was immediate and incriminating.

> [5] *David burned with anger against the man and said to Nathan, "As surely as the LORD lives, the man who did this deserves to die!*
> [6] *He must pay for that lamb four times over, because he did such a thing and* **had no pity.**"

2 Samuel 12:5-6, emphasis added.

Well might David burn with righteous indignation, make reference to the Lord, and deplore such a brutal and insensitive action by the rich man. But it was not for long.

> [7] *Then Nathan said to David,* "**You are the man**! *This is what the LORD, the God of Israel, says: 'I anointed you king over Israel, and I delivered you from the hand of Saul.*

*⁸I gave your master's house to you, and **your master's wives into your arms**. I gave you the house of Israel and Judah. **And if all this had been too little, I would have given you even more.***
*⁹**Why did you despise the word of the LORD** by doing what is evil in his eyes? **You struck down Uriah the Hittite with the sword and took his wife to be your own**. You killed him with the sword of the Ammonites.*

2 Samuel 12:7-9, emphases added.

Not one of the King's finer moments!! If that rich man deserved to die, David had no defence for his own actions—he should die. And he had all that he needed in terms of wives and concubines. But he was consumed by lust with no reference to God's generous provision and capacity to give even more.

David came to admit that whatever he did wrong in regard to Bathsheba and Uriah, ultimately his sin was against God.

*¹³Then David said to Nathan, "**I have sinned against the LORD.**"*

2 Samuel 12:13, emphasis added.

He later lamented in one of his Psalms:

*³For I know my transgressions, and **my sin is always before me.***
*⁴**Against you, you only, have I sinned** and done what is evil in your sight,*

Psalm 51:3, 4, emphasis added.

But in the short term, God's judgment was on David, and the child died.

It is instructive to read the whole of Psalm 51, captioned as written after his encounter with Nathan the prophet in the context of his adultery. It shows the depth of grief and repentance that came to him having been faced with the truth of his situation.

This is a Scripture—together with the whole episode—that we can recall in our own circumstances. The Word of God is crucial. If only David had been as devotional before the event.

Fundamental—keeping close accounts with God. Guard the devotional life at all costs—or pay the price!

It is futile to try to work out our own fleshly pursuits.

Be instructed from God's Word:

> ^{5}*Trust in the LORD with all your heart and **lean not on your own understanding**;*
> ^{6}*in all your ways acknowledge him, and **he will make your paths** straight.*
>
> Proverbs 3:5-6, emphases added.

c) CORRECTIVE CASE: JOSEPH.

By way of contrast to King David, we might recall the example of Joseph, who in a foreign country and with no one to report on him, remained faithful to God, and respected Potiphar's wife and her husband (Genesis 39:1-6). Mrs Potiphar had tried to seduce Joseph, but he was *alert* and *aware* of the presence of God in that remote place in Egypt, far from his family:

> ^{7}*and after a while his master's wife took notice of Joseph and said, "**Come to bed with me!**"*
> ^{8}*But **he refused**. "With me in charge," he told her, "my master does not concern himself with anything in the house; everything he owns he has entrusted to my care.*
> ^{9}*No one is greater in this house than I am. My master has withheld nothing from me except you, because you are his wife. **How then could I do such a wicked thing and sin against God?**"*
>
> Genesis 39:7-9, emphases added.

Could Joseph have sinned? Of course he could. But as a man living in the presence of God, could he have sinned? Impossible!

An awareness of God's Word prepares us for a wide range of circumstances that might take us off guard, but we are not off guard with regard to the Word of God, and like Joseph, we can rely on that devotional awareness.

Many a man would not hesitate to take up the option that Mrs Potiphar offered. There was no need for Joseph to advance a plan. And there was no one to know, being thousands of kilometres from home, and no Sunday school teacher looking over his shoulder. But there was God.

As noted above as we looked at King David's life, the following Proverb illustrates the principle that was no doubt before Joseph:

> [21]*For a **man's ways are in full view of the LORD**, and he examines all his paths.*
>
> Proverbs 5:21.

Joseph's life was lived before his holy God—eliminating the possibility of sin. This attitude that reflects the character of the true Christian is described by Dr John Meigs, the headmaster of The Hill School attended by missionary William Borden, in the following terms (Taylor 1980, 23, emphases added):

> … the test of [the young Christian's] religious life is what he **is** and what he **does** when he is **not** on his knees in prayer, **not** reading his Bible, **not** listening to good preachers and **not** participating in religious meetings.

d) THE EXAMPLE OF JESUS.

When Jesus was tempted by the devil, He could quote the Scriptures by way of refuting the devil's deception at each of his three temptations (Matthew 4:1-11):

¹Then Jesus was led by the Spirit into the desert to be tempted by the devil ...
³The tempter came to him and said ...
*⁴Jesus answered, "**It is written** ...*
⁵Then the devil took him to the holy city ...
⁶"If you are the Son of God" ...
*⁷Jesus answered him, "**It is also written**:*
⁸Again, the devil took him ...
*¹⁰Jesus said to him, "Away from me, Satan! For **it is written**:*

Matthew 4:1-10, emphases added.

The Scriptures are replete with examples from which we can be helped—but we need to study it to be aware.

A knowledge of the Scriptures will be the basis for deliberate choices NOT to sin. We are responsible for doing this regular preparation. A knowledge of the Scriptures will also help us avoid developing habitual behaviours which are displeasing to God.

**NOTE: CRUCIAL: the devotional Life.

3) ACCOUNTABILITY

As a general principle of Christian discipleship, it is exceedingly helpful to have a **regular prayer partner**. There is the opportunity to consistently share with a confidante who can give support and encouragement—and it is reciprocal/mutual.

This method is particularly helpful in the area of dealing with **habit sins** where there is the process of recovery, and of learning new responses, and adopting constructive behaviours. Also, as a defence to help avoid new strategies that are destined to form new and equally evil habits.

As a single secondary school teacher in my first country appointment, I benefitted greatly from sharing with another new teacher in similar circumstances—as we reflected on our new church experiences, accommodation arrangements, desires for the future (including matrimonial expectations), occasional difficulties and struggles, etc. We also jointly led some boys' weekend Christian camps.

The most important aspect was the fact that there was always an immediate reference point for any issue that we were facing individually. We did not have to wait until a matter was out of control before reluctantly seeking help. As we met each week we were able to keep on top of any matters, to discuss it/them, and to pray together. And we could always meet for extra times of sharing if necessary.

Some type of accountability is very helpful in overcoming defeat in the area of sin. We noted above how my chocoholic daughter was helped to work through her "addiction". It is a regular method used for recovering alcoholics.

And it is particularly beneficial when the other party is able to identify sympathetically—whether an ex-criminal, rehabilitating murderer, or an habitual liar. My case with the school-teacher friend meant that we both understood each other perfectly. An alcoholic is going to more easily be helped by someone else who is also an ex-alcoholic, being able to identify with all the temptations and desires. And no doubt best equipped to help with monitoring a graded process of achieving victory over the temptation.

One area I found particularly applicable in needing accountability monitoring, was for Christians seeking to extract themselves from the habit of using **pornographic literature**—a far more common complaint than we might be aware! The very nature of the problem is usually clandestine and secretive, and left to their own devices victims often struggle, with many relapses. Accountability can help monitor any relapses without expecting immediate success, but encouraging the increasing number of weeks between any lapses, giving a **graded sense of achievement**.

5.5.2 COMMENTS ON EACH OF THE THREE CATEGORIES OF SIN

1) DELIBERATE SIN

With deliberate sin, we have made a deliberate choice, and to our shame it was the wrong one. We don't have to replicate that.

Deliberate sin can be put in the category of "one-offs".

In the conquest of Canaan under Joshua, as they attacked Ai (Joshua 7:1-26), Achan (as we noted earlier) committed an impromptu "one-off" sin (i.e. not premeditated or habitual):

> *²¹When **I saw** in the plunder a beautiful robe from Babylonia, two hundred shekels of silver and a wedge of gold weighing fifty shekels, **I coveted** them **and took** them.*
>
> Joshua 7:21, emphases added.

It was a single sin—by deliberate consent of the will—with devastating results, but it was "opportunistic" rather than a regular or habitual sin.

It is when one "one-off" becomes repeated over a period of time that it may develop into a habit that may result in a person becoming, for example, a kleptomaniac—"a person who helps himself because he can't help himself!" That then moves to the third category here, **Habit sin**, see below.

But how to deal with deliberate sin.

Firstly, there is the matter of **attitude and the mind**. This particular issue was addressed in the general considerations given in the "common ground" section, (#5.5.1), and has great benefit for **deliberate sin**, in that we need to understand the nature of our problem in the context of God's Word. The principles and truths of God's Word become the reference point for our decisions—as for Joseph.

If tempted to lust for something, we might well recall the story of Achan that we noted earlier. He made no reference to God or His principles, but looked only at the objects.

If faced with the opportunity of sexual infidelity or selfish gratification, we might well remember the story of King David, and be warned by his failure in pursuing Bathsheba, and having her husband Uriah killed in the process (2 Samuel 11). Again, he only looked at the object of his lust, and pursued that at whatever cost.

We would be better instructed to look at the example of Joseph, and be inspired to affirm his statement in the face of temptation: ***How then could I do such a wicked thing and sin against God?***

Secondly, there is the matter of **making the actual choices—the operation of the consenting will.**

Fresh from the presence of God, and with His Word ringing in our ears, we need to pause long enough to commit the situation to the Lord, and to make the decision—**deliberately**—in His presence. Like Joseph did. Like Jesus Himself did.

Repeated practice of this spiritual exercise will help us to be bold in our rejection of Satan's attacks.

Be strong and make deliberate, positive choices.

OVERALL re DELIBERATE SIN:

- We must know our areas of weakness, and be more on the alert.

- We need to develop strategies to assist us in gaining step-by-step victories. And as the old hymn says: "Each victory will help you some other to win", and

  Ask the Saviour to help you.
  Comfort strengthen and keep you;
  He is willing to aid you—

He will carry you through.

Yield Not to Temptation.

- We need to maintain a consistent and balanced devotional life that keeps our subconscious mind dedicated to the principles and attitudes from God's Word.
- We need to be assertive in our decision-making, and not allow other people or circumstances to dictate to us how we are to behave.

**NOTE: concerning sins of omission.

It is not only things that we have **done**, that can be deliberate sins, but there are things that we may have left **undone** that might also constitute sin, because by default—and therefore a choice—we have sinned:

> [17]*Anyone, then, who knows the good he ought to do and **doesn't do it, sins.***

James 4:17, emphasis added.

Likewise, we have a responsibility to act in the circumstances in which God has placed us:

> [27]*Do not withhold good from those who deserve it, when it is in your power to act.*

Proverbs 3:27.

And by extension, any failure to act—and thus a sin of omission—betrays our true spiritual condition:

> [17]*If anyone has material possessions and sees his brother in need but has no pity on him,* **how can the love of God be in him***?*

1 John 3:17, emphasis added.

Such an omission raises a question over whether we are in fact Christians. If God's love is not in us, why?

2) UNWITTING SIN

In one sense it is impossible to "deal with unwitting sins", or to adequately prepare for them.

- At very least, we can make sure that we maintain our devotional life. That will give us a raised sense of awareness of anything possibly being wrong—but we may still unwittingly "walk on the grass"!

- Maintaining right relationships, and being prepared and alert for the unexpected, will help:

    > [8]*Be **self-controlled and alert**. Your enemy the devil prowls around like a roaring lion looking for someone to devour.*
    >
    > 1 Peter 5:8, emphasis added.

- Additionally, **know** your enemy (the devil) and his devices, and be prepared without being paranoid.

    > [11]*in order that Satan might not outwit us. For **we are not unaware of his schemes.***
    >
    > 2 Corinthians 2:11, emphasis added.

3) HABIT SIN

This is the pivotal area, for the most common problems with sins.

Deliberate sins are clearly our responsibility and our fault—notwithstanding all the nonsense about "sin natures" or other personalised third party determinative entities.

Unwitting sins are completely unpredictable and there is minimal preparation or avoidance that we can exercise.

But habit sins cause the greatest difficulties and dilemmas for most Christians.

And so once again we must note Paul's dilemma:

> *[15]I do not understand what I do. For what I want to do I do not do, but what I hate I do.*
> *[16]And if I do what I do not want to do, I agree that the law is good.*
> *[17]As it is, it is no longer I myself who do it, but it is sin living in me*
> *[18]I know that nothing good lives in me, that is, in my sinful nature. For **I have the desire to do what is good, but I cannot carry it out.***
> *[19]For what I do is not the good I want to do; no, the evil I do not want to do—this I keep on doing.*
> *[20]Now if I do what I do not want to do, it is no longer I who do it, but it is sin living in me that does it.*
> *[24]**What a wretched man I am!** Who will rescue me from this body of death?*
>
> Romans 7:15-20, 24, emphases added.

We have already clearly noted that this dilemma is nothing to do with "sin natures" or otherwise. The chart at #4.2.1 demonstrates that there are only these three categories of sin. Once that is established, we can narrow the whole debate down and address the real issue.

Habit sins occur when least expected, and quite spontaneously. Therefore it is important to be able to identify where and when these situations might occur. It may be necessary—at least initially—to avoid areas of problem. Don't go near a bar, if alcohol is your problem. Don't be alone at a sports event if there is likely to be stress and arguments, that could lead to altercations and fights. Don't go alone to a smorgasbord restaurant if eating is a problem. At the start.

Make sure that in all these circumstances you have someone to assist with accountability and support.

The Apostle John, like Paul, addresses this problem of "ongoing" sin. **Habitual** sins are completely contrary to the New Man condition. John suggests that to *continue* in sin is virtually an impossibility for a Christian. In fact, if someone does "go on sinning" he pronounces himself a non-Christian!—that person *has (n)either seen Him or known Him* (verse 6, below). Of course we will all sin from time to time, but **habitual sin** amounts to rebellion against God as we noted earlier (1 John 3:4):

> [4]*Everyone who sins* **(goes on sinning)** *breaks the law; in fact, sin is lawlessness.*
> [5]*But you know that he appeared so that he might take away our sins. And in Him is no sin.*
> [6]**No one who lives in Him keeps on sinning. No one who continues to sin has either seen Him or known Him.** [Not even saved!]
> [7]*Dear children, do not let anyone lead you astray. He who does what is right is righteous, just as he is righteous.*
> [8]*He who does what is sinful is of the devil, because the devil has been sinning from the beginning. The reason the Son of God appeared was to destroy the devil's work.*
> [9]**No one who is born of God will continue to sin**, *because God's seed remains in him;* **he cannot go on sinning, because he has been born of God.**
> [18]**We know that anyone born of God does not continue to sin;** *the one who was born of God keeps him safe, and the evil one cannot harm him.*
>
> 1 John 3:4-9: 5:18, emphases added.

When a Christian sins, he should be immediately aware of it and address it, as John clearly enjoins, because:

> [7] *... if we walk in the light, as he is in the light, we have fellowship with one another, and the blood of Jesus, his Son, purifies us from all sin.* (1 John 1:7).

Walking in the light, will immediately show-up any sin or sinful intention, and having become aware of sin, the Christian will seek to confess and repudiate it, receiving God's forgiveness (1 John 1:9):

> [9]*If we confess our sins, he is faithful and just and will forgive us our sins and purify us from all unrighteousness.*

It is when a Christian has so adopted and learned habit sins (as a Christian) that the greatest difficulty arises. He is not aware that he has sinned, or like Paul he becomes aware when it is all too late, and he cries out in despair, *"I keep on doing what I don't want to do, and I don't do what I want. Who will deliver me from this body of death?"*

It doesn't have to happen. We are not under obligation to serve sin. So yield yourselves to God.

And so the correctives, which are the same as for deliberate sins, but here there needs to be strong corrective behaviours as well. How will you react next time someone steps on your toe? I.e. RELEARN reactions and so develop "habits" of grace and gentleness.

But even then, we can't accomplish this ourselves. See the note re Jesus and His ability to perform, below.

Certainly Paul cries out in despair:

[24]What a wretched man I am! Who will rescue me from this body of death?

Romans 7:24.

But then with rejoicing he exclaims:

*[25]Thanks be to God—**through Jesus Christ our Lord**! So then, I myself in my mind am a slave to God's law, but in the sinful nature* (sic) *a slave to the law of sin.*

Romans 7:25, emphasis added.

Who will help me? God will.

It is a spiritual battle, and if we consent to the Spirit (walk in the Spirit) the impulses associated with the flesh will not be fulfilled—but negated (Gibson n.d., 3):

*[16]So I say, **live by the Spirit**, and you will not gratify the desires of the sinful nature* (sic) [flesh]. (Galatians 5:16, emphasis added).

We need God's help, as Paul makes very clear:

¹³For if you live according to the sinful nature (sic) [flesh], *you will die; but if **by the Spirit you put to death the misdeeds** [practices] **of the body,** you will live,*

Romans 8:13, emphasis added.

It is only possible through the assistance of the Spirit, but He acts in response to our consenting will. John Owen made the incisive comment (1996, 22-23):

> ... but this is the work of the Spirit; by him alone it is to be wrought, and by no other power is it to be brought about. Mortification from a self-strength, carried on by ways of self-invention, unto the end of a self-righteousness, is the soul and substance of all false religion in the world ...

And don't feel that our inability to achieve victory over the **habit** (practice) is a sign of defeat, because Jesus acknowledged His limitations. Note the following.

**NOTE: Jesus' ability to perform:

There are a number of verses in John's Gospel, where Jesus unashamedly declares His absolute dependence on His Father, and His consuming desire, only to do His Father's will. Jesus operated with a consenting will to His Father.

> *¹⁹Jesus gave them this answer: "I tell you the truth, the Son **can do nothing by himself; he can do only what he sees his Father doing,** because whatever the Father does the Son also does.*
> *³⁰**By myself I can do nothing**; I judge only as I hear, and my judgment is just, for I seek not to please myself but him who sent me.*

John 5: 19, 30, emphases added.

> *¹⁶Jesus answered, "**My teaching is not my own**. It comes from him who sent me.*

John 7:16, emphasis added.

*²⁸So Jesus said, "When you have lifted up the Son of Man, then you will know that I am the one I claim to be and that **I do nothing on my own** but speak just what the Father has taught me.*

John 8:28, emphasis added.

*⁴²Jesus said to them, "If God were your Father, you would love me, for I came from God and now am here. **I have not come on my own**; but he sent me.*

John 8: 42, emphasis added.

This fact of Jesus' operation was acknowledged by the man born blind who received his sight:

*³³If this man were not from God, **he could do nothing.**"*

John 9:33, emphasis added.

On this evidence, Jesus indicated that because the Father does the works, anyone who has faith in Christ, would be able to do the works that Jesus did, and even greater.

*¹²I tell you the truth, **anyone who has faith in me will do what I have been doing. He will do even greater things than these**, because I am going to the Father.*

John 14:12, emphasis added.

OVERALL re HABIT SINS:

- COMMON GROUND Keep these areas, noted in the Introduction (#5.5.1), in perspective here, as for all the categories of sin.

- PLAN CORRECTIVE BEHAVIOURS. Over against the **deliberate sins, deliberately** cultivate corrective behaviours. Think of the areas of failure in the light of God's Word and its principles. Think of ways to precisely avoid the situations that precipitate the habit responses. Think of alternative ways of responding to those situations. Cry out "Hallelujah!" if you hit your finger instead of cursing.

- IDENTIFY AREAS OF WEAKNESS. You know from past experience where the habit sins have occurred, so be particularly on the alert when approaching that situation. For example, you are going to a restaurant, and that is the scene of much past unthinking gluttony. Deliberately commit the situation to God and ask for His help.

- ACCOUNTABILITY. Address the fact that you are approaching this area of difficulty, and tell one of your friends who will also be going, "Keep an eye on me, and help me to keep a good balance".

- DEFINE PARAMETERS. Demark the area of the habit sin. In this case, select only sufficient food for your needs. Place that on your plate and show your friend. Stop and make a note. Eat only that amount irrespective of other pressures, and keep your friend nearby to support you.

* * * * *

CHAPTER 6

CONCLUSIONS

Let us summarise the situation.

6.1 THE OLD MAN IS DEAD.

Never again will he "rear his ugly head". He is crucified with Christ. He has no power over our present situation.

6.2 CLARIFY THE TERMS.

There is no such thing as a "sin nature" or "corrupt nature".

The "flesh" is the human flesh with its normal healthy appetites. Of themselves they are no problem. The problem is when we seek to gratify these desires as ends in themselves.

6.3 THE NEW MAN.

This is the new condition having "put off" the Old Man, at the same time "putting on the New Man". This is the new life in Christ, in which we need to grow in sanctification.

6.4 INCULCATED HABITS.

It is essential to recognise this area as delineated by Paul in Romans 7. This is the primary source of dilemmas and disillusionment in the Christian experience. If we can isolate this category of sin, we have just about won the battle.

6.5 DEVOTIONAL LIFE.

It is fundamental, essential, pivotal, crucial, and many other words, to protect and maintain an effective devotional life. It is in the "attitude of your minds"—the things that you think on and reflect on, that are the source of your external behaviours

6.6 ACCEPTING RESPONSIBILITY.

Pivotal to the whole matter of sin, is the operation of the **will**. The will is never an entity that can be contaminated or corrupted. It is a determination based on the information in the mind, issuing in decisions as we decide—whether good or bad. Again, protect the mind with the devotional life.

The Old Man is DEAD!

NEVER to rise again.

And I am responsible for my sin.

* * * * *

BIBLIOGRAPHY

Bagster, S (publisher). n.d. *Analytical Greek Lexicon.* Bagster, London.

Barclay, W. 1958. *The Letters to the Galatians and the Ephesians.* St Andrew Press, Edinburgh.

Barth, K. 1956. G.W. Bromiley (trans.). *Church Dogmatics. 4. The Doctrine of Reconciliation Part 1.* T. & T. Clark, Edinburgh.

Berkhof, L. (rev'd) 1949. *Systematic Theology.* Eerdmans, Grand Rapids.

Brunner, E. 1952. *The Christian Doctrine of Creation and Redemption. Dogmatics 2.* Lutterworth, London.

Bultmann, R. 1952. *Theology of the New Testament* 1. SCM, London.

Criswell, W.A. 1973. The Baptism, Filling and Gifts of the Holy Spirit. Zondervan, Grand Rapids.

Cross, F.L. (ed.) *Studia Evangelica II.* Akademie-Verlag, Berlin.

Dieter, M.E., Hoekema, A.A., Horton, S.M., *et al.* 1987. *Five Views on Sanctification.* Zondervan, Grand Rapids.

Dunn, J.D.G. 1975a. *Jesus and the Spirit.* SCM, London.

Dunn, J.D.G. 1975b. Romans 7:14-25 in the Theology of Paul. *Theologische Zeitschrift.* 31, 257-273.

Gibson, E.G. n.d *The Old Man and the New Man,* paper prepared for student classes at Queensland Baptist Theological College.

Gordon, A.J. (1894) Reprinted 1949. *The Ministry of the Holy Spirit*. Judson Press, Philadelphia.

Guthrie, D. 1981. *New Testament Theology*. IVP, Illinois.

Higgins, A.J.B. 1959. Ed. *New Testament Essays*. Manchester University Press, Manchester.

Hoekema, A.A. 1987. The Reformed Perspective. M.E. Dieter, A.A. Hoekema, S.M. Horton, et al. *Five Views on Sanctification*. Zondervan, Grand Rapids.

Ingram, G.S. 1964. *The Fullness of the Holy Spirit*. Christian Literature Crusade, London.

Keil, C.F. & Delitzsch, F. 1980. The Pentateuch. C.F. Keil, & F. Delitzsch. *Commentary on the Old Testament in Ten Volumes*, various translators. Eerdmans, Grand Rapids, 1, Trans. James Martin.

Keil, C.F. & Delitzsch, F. 1980. *Commentary on the Old Testament in Ten Volumes*, various translators. Eerdmans, Grand Rapids.

Lewis, C.S. 1940. *The Problem of Pain*. Centenary Press, London.

Lloyd-Jones, D.M. 1942. *The Plight of Man and the Power of God*. Pickering & Inglis, London.

Manson, W. 1959. Notes on the Argument of Romans (chapters 1-8). A.J.B. Higgins (ed.). *New Testament Essays*. Manchester University Press, Manchester. 150-164.

Morris, L. 1960. *Spirit of the Living God*. I.V.F., London.

Moule, C.F.D. 1973. "The New Life" in Colossians 3:1-17. *Review and Expositor,* LXX, 4, Fall 1973.

Otto, R.E. 1990. *The Solidarity of Mankind in Jonathan Edwards' Doctrine of Original Sin*. The Evangelical Quarterly. 62 (3), July 1990, 205-221.

Owen, J. 1996. *The Mortification of Sin.* Christian Focus Publications Ltd, Scotland, Great Britain.

Packer, J.I. 1964. The "Wretched Man" in Romans 7, F.L. Cross (ed.) *Studia Evangelica II.* Akademie-Verlag, Berlin. 621-7.

Ridgway, J.M. 1978. The Pauline Treatment of Sarx as a Spiritual Liability. *The Tyndale Paper.* 23 (3), July.

Robertson, A.T. 1931. *Word Pictures in the New Testament.* 4. Broadman, Nashville.

Smith, C.R. 1983. Two Natures—or One? *Voice.* 62. July-August. Pp. 19-21.

Stibbs, A.M. 1959. *God's Church.* I.V.F., London.

Strong, A.H. 1907. *Systematic Theology.* Pickering and Inglis, London.

Strong, J. 1996. *The Exhaustive Concordance of the Bible*: (electronic ed.). Woodside Bible Fellowship, Ontario.

Swincer, D.A. 2011a. *Condemned Already.* Integrity Publications, Adelaide, South Australia.

Swincer, D.A. 2011b. *Tongues: Confused by Ecstasy.* Integrity Publications, Adelaide, South Australia.

Swincer, D.A. 2015. *Let God Speak: His Word is Authority.* Integrity Publications, Adelaide, South Australia.

Swincer, D.A. 2016a. *Tongues: Genuine Biblical Language.* Integrity Publications, Adelaide, South Australia.

Swincer, D.A. 2016b (2nd ed'n). *Will Nobody Listen?* Integrity Publications, Adelaide, South Australia.

Swincer, D.A. 2019. *Prayer: Premised on Worship.* Integrity Publications, Adelaide, South Australia.

Taylor, H. 1980. *William Borden.* Moody Press, Chicago.

Taylor, R.S. 1945 (rev'd). *A Right Conception of Sin.* Beacon Hill Press, USA.

Thomas, I. 1964. *The Saving Life of Christ.* Zondervan, Great Britain.

Vine, W. E., Unger, M. F., & White, W., 1996. *Vine's Complete Expository Dictionary Of Old and New Testament Words.* T. Nelson, Nashville.

Wilson, A.S. n.d. *Concerning Complexities Paradoxes and Perils.* Mimeographed copy, no details.

* * * * *

APPENDIX
MY GRANDFATHER'S CLOCK

Henry Clay Work - 1876

(Copyright Unknown).

My grandfather's clock was too large for the shelf,
So it stood ninety years on the floor;
It was taller by half than the old man himself,
Though it weighed not a pennyweight more.
It was bought on the morn of the day that he was born,
And was always his treasure and pride;
But it stopped short — never to go again —
When the old man died.

> Ninety years without slumbering
> (tick, tock, tick, tock),
> His life's seconds numbering,
> (tick, tock, tick, tock),
> It stopped short — never to go again —
> When the old man died.

In watching its pendulum swing to and fro,
Many hours had he spent while a boy;
And in childhood and manhood the clock seemed to know
And to share both his grief and his joy.
For it struck twenty-four when he entered at the door,
With a blooming and beautiful bride;

But it stopped short — never to go again —
When the old man died.

> Ninety years without slumbering
> (tick, tock, tick, tock),
> His life's seconds numbering,
> (tick, tock, tick, tock),
> It stopped short — never to go again —
> When the old man died.

My grandfather said that of those he could hire,
Not a servant so faithful he found;
For it wasted no time, and had but one desire —
At the close of each week to be wound.
And it kept in its place — not a frown upon its face,
And its hands never hung by its side.
But it stopped short — never to go again —
When the old man died.

> Ninety years without slumbering
> (tick, tock, tick, tock),
> His life's seconds numbering,
> (tick, tock, tick, tock),
> It stopped short — never to go again —
> When the old man died.

It rang an alarm in the dead of the night —
An alarm that for years had been dumb;
And we knew that his spirit was pluming for flight —
That his hour of departure had come.
Still the clock kept the time, with a soft and muffled chime,
As we silently stood by his side;
But it stopped short — never to go again —
When the old man died.

Ninety years without slumbering
(tick, tock, tick, tock),
His life's seconds numbering,
(tick, tock, tick, tock),
It stopped short — never to go again —
When the old man died.

* * * * *

BIOGRAPHICAL SKETCH

BACKGROUND, TRAINING

Rev Dr David A Swincer is an ordained Baptist Minister, having served almost 40 years in pastoral ministry, including 13 years as a seminary professor.

Raised on a sheep farm in South Australia, David developed a strong sense of the practicalities of life, and this experience has been invaluable in his pastoral and lecturing experience.

He originally trained as a secondary school teacher, specializing in mathematics and science. He acquired a B.A. degree and Secondary Teaching Diploma. He taught for 4 years full-time.

The unmistakable call to Pastoral Ministry led to training in the New South Wales Baptist Theological Seminary, where he did post-graduate study, gaining a B.D. and Dip. R.E. After 8 years of Pastoral Ministry, he moved to the Seminary Position, specializing in New Testament – especially Greek exegesis. Circumstances meant that he also lectured widely in other areas, undertaking some lecturing in O.T. exegesis, Modern Church History, overview of theology, and a special emphasis in pastoral subjects (including writing several papers on associated topics, notably a Pre-marriage Counselling Course; Marriage Enrichment; Conflict resolution).

He pursued strong personal interest in the nature and practice of worship.

A pastor at heart, Dr Swincer loved to see the practical side of careful exegesis and theological education.

During this time he undertook M.A. and Doctoral studies.

His whole ministry has been marked by a willingness to think laterally, and to challenge common presuppositions, in the search for the truth. His books strongly challenge traditional positions that seem to be held unthinkingly. That will be a challenge to the reader!

MINISTRY

Dr Swincer served in pastoral ministry for nine years before moving into seminary education for 13 years. During the latter part of that time he simultaneously pastored a church before returning to the full-time pastoral ministry – an extra 18 years. In addition, there have been several interim pastorates.

During the years of Seminary teaching especially, there was the opportunity to visit many churches, to address teaching weekends in a variety of circumstances, to speak at weekend family and Youth camps, and teaching conventions – all of which provided a rich appreciation of people in all types of circumstances, with counselling problems from theological misunderstandings or practical insensitivities.

Coupled with research and study, he had the opportunity to travel and to undertake several preaching/teaching/evangelistic tours. All these opportunities have provided a rich and diverse background of experience that equips him for the balance of theological and practical writing which has always been simmering in the background.

* * * * *

SEE BELOW.

FURTHER READING
SEE BELOW

TONGUES: VOLUME 1
CONFUSED BY ECSTASY

Dr. Swincer has done a monumental service to the Christian world. Addressing a topic that is often poorly understood, or bitterly divisive, he has sought to remove the assumptions – in particular, the presumed precursor of ecstasy – from the biblical teaching about the Gift of Tongues for the Church. He carefully distinguishes between the one-stage phenomenon of the Book of the Acts, and the two-stage phenomenon of the gift for the Church.

The contemporary background of ecstasy in the Mystery Religions of the first century and beyond, is very significant in appreciating the nature of the biblical gift.

Of particular personal interest to me, was his careful tracing of the historic roots of tongue-speaking in the various denominations. This alone deserves wide publicity, as it is often very poorly understood, and usually quite prejudicial.

There are many historic traces of teachings and developments that show remarkable research and high academic excellence.

This should become a text-book on the subject.

Dr Clifford Wilson – prolific author and Christian statesman, Australia.

* * * * *

**Available at the website:
www.integritypublications.biz

SEE MORE BELOW:

CONDEMNED ALREADY

I highly commend the propositions espoused in this book. The problems associated with the Doctrine of Original Sin and its ramifications for the ministry of Evangelism are seldom appreciated, and certainly not adequately addressed. This book presents a view that is soundly biblical, and theologically helpful in the resolution of many of the problems – such as Alien Guilt, the Causative Sin in each of our own experiences, and the matters of our personal responsibility and accountability.

I warmly commend it to be carefully assessed.

Dr EG Gibson – one-time principal of the Baptist Theological Seminary of Queensland, Australia.

* * * * *

**Available at the website:
www.integritypublications.biz

SEE MORE BELOW:

WILL NOBODY LISTEN?

How embarrassingly obvious!

Two simple aspects of regular counselling/interviewing, brought together in a unique relationship and the results are nothing short of astonishing. We all interview two parties separately—at least from time to time. And we all write notes of some description. But this method of combining these two methods, very discreetly, and with great attention to details and as a clear tool of communication between two parties at odds, is simply enlightening.

Conflict Resolution is not new—but this combination certainly seems to be. Dr Swincer should be deeply thanked for this timely and very effective emphasis.

During more than forty years in the pastoral (and associated) ministries, I have been able to benefit from these methodologies to great advantage, and so I have no hesitation in warmly commending this volume to pastors in particular, but also to anyone involved in counselling ministries, especially where there is a focus on Conflict Resolution.

Those who employ this methodology will have great success personally, but perhaps more importantly, difficult situations will be remarkably solved, and warring factions brought to happy resolution.

Let there be more fulfilling reconciliation!

A Seasoned Pastor – having enjoyed the blessings of seeing families in particular, brought to peace.
**Available at the website: www.integritypublications.biz

SEE BELOW

DAVID A SWINCER

LET GOD SPEAK
HIS WORD IS AUTHORITY

LET GOD SPEAK:
HIS WORD IS AUTHORITY
A PERSONAL TESTIMONY

Praise God for this book. Brilliant!

During my theological training, I studied exegesis for four years, with an average of 4 semester hours of lectures each week. At the end of the studies, I could only throw all my notes into the trash.

Nothing that was said established a methodology for doing exegesis nor how to record it for the future.

Interestingly, it was on my annual vacation with the family at the end of my first exit year of pastoral ministry, that I discovered what exegesis was all about. I had taken Kenneth Wuest's Word Series book *First Peter in the Greek New Testament* to use in my devotions each day. I was amazed to find the simple significance of the Greek in order to understand the bible.

I was suddenly brimming with information that I desperately wished to keep at my fingertips, but how to record it in a readily accessible form. And so the search for a methodology.

Dr Swincer's book explains clearly why the bible is authoritative, how it should be interpreted, and then how to use it in the ministry of preaching and teaching through careful exegesis for my contemporary situation. But the cream on the cake, is a model for a methodology of how to cumulatively record the fruit of my labours in preparation. Brilliant!

**Available at the website:
www.integritypublications.biz
SEE BELOW

TONGUES: VOLUME 2
GENUINE BIBLICAL LANGUAGE

UNIQUE! This is the only biblical construct that even remotely attempts to identify the biblical criteria and then to apply them to a practical application. The mountain of arguments about all the facets of glossolalia are mostly hot air that don't even touch the real issues, and nothing constructive results. This book gives a clear outline of the biblical criteria, identifies the historical precedents and background, and then draws these together in a construct of Genuine Biblical Languages.

A retired pastor comments:

"This book by David Swincer is a demonstration of close and thorough exegesis. You will be rewarded with many insights and pastoral tips as you read this work thoughtfully and reflectively. This work is also a good example of approaching Scripture seriously and wrestling with its application - sadly, by and large, a lost art today."

Mark Ingram.

**Available at the website:
www.integritypublications.biz

SEE BELOW

David A Swincer

The Old Man Died

My Grandfathers Clock
It stopped short,
never to go again when
The Old Man Died

Sequel to "Condemned Already"

THE OLD MAN DIED

I am most appreciative of the fundamental concepts that are espoused in *The Old Man Died*. Smith, Murray and Gibson—referred to in the book—are three of the few authors who have been prepared to state the biblical position—or anything remotely near it—and this is a most refreshing read.

Likewise, Dr Swincer certainly has the ability to "think laterally" in regard to biblical doctrines. There has been an "habitual response" to the concepts of the "sin nature", and the "flesh" that as Dr Swincer explains, have become ingrained in the theological mind-set.

The broad use of Scripture and its exegetical application is masterly.

In addition to the insightful correctives, Dr Swincer shows a truly pastoral heart in seeking to help people at large in the Christian community, who continually struggle in the area that can only be described as "habitual sin".

Thank you.

Arthur S.

(A pastor with a strong practical theological application).

* * * * *

**Available at the website:
www.integritypublications.biz

SEE MORE BELOW:

COMING: READY OR NOT

Eschatology lends itself to all manner of dogmatic assertions and beliefs. In this book, *COMING: READY OR NOT,* those assertions are present, but they are well substantiated.

Most significantly, from my experience as a professional lecturer, the careful basis of the whole concept of eschatology and its premise on the declared Word of God—as given in this book—and especially the clear emphasis on a literal hermeneutic, gives the conclusions a cogency seldom given in books on the subject.

Consequently, the comprehensive topic of the Kingdom of God—almost unique in a discussion of this type—is brilliant in its clarity of the overall plan of God, giving a perspective to eschatology that is most enlightening. To see the concept of "this world order" that Dr Swincer uses, to see the beginning and the end, from the creation to the consummation, is a noteworthy approach to understanding eschatology, especially as it locks in to God's original purpose for the creation.

Extending from this overview, is the importance of God's people Israel. Petty argument cannot address this issue, and the pervasive references to Israel throughout Scripture, from Old Testament to New Testament, are best appreciated in the significant role recognised for these people as demonstrated in this book.

A "must read" volume.

A retired professor of New Testament.

**Available at the website:

www.integritypublications.biz

* * * * *

SEE BELOW:

HOMOSEXUAL TERRORISM

RAINBOW PERVERSION

Bi-sexuals Dykes GAYS Sodomites Pansexuals LESBIANS Fags Queers Androphiles Transsexuals Intersex

DAVID A SWINCER

HOMOSEXUAL TERRORISM:
Rainbow Perversion

Have you heard of "gay cakes"? This is a picture of those who for conscience (in the US) would not provide "cakes", i.e. cater for a gay marriage reception, **once the "marriage" equality laws had come in.** Immediately the gay lobby sued for discrimination and the owner (Aaron Klein) was forced to comply or be fined—in this case $135,000—and put out of business.

This is the work of a terrorist mentality. No consideration for anyone else's beliefs. No respect for other universally and well-established views. Just force with coercive pressure to demand conformity to their narrow and perverted ideology.

The "marriage" equality debate is a ruse to have laws enacted that will then open the floodgates for all manner of perversion, followed by discrimination laws to force the perverse views on the apathetic public.

Only 1% of the population is trying to manipulate the 99%, and we are just letting it happen. There is an urgency to acquaint everybody with the situation before we lose the opportunity to have a say. If we delay, it will not be just a matter of "gay cakes", a pastor will not be able to refuse to "marry" a gay couple. A church will not be able to refuse the use of its facilities for a gay reception. These things are already happening in Canada, USA, UK, Ireland, and other places that have allowed gay "marriage" to be introduced.

And it won't be a matter of tolerating these changes, the new deconstructionism of "toleration" requires hearty assent and approval of the aberrations.

* * * * *

**Available at the website: www.integritypublications.biz

SHEPHERDING GOD'S FLOCK
LEADERSHIP MINISTRY IN THE CHURCH

The traditional pastoral role has changed over the last decades, largely due to the growth of mega-churches. The senior pastor has tended to become more an executive leader with an emphasis on public preaching as the figurehead of a large organisation.

The traditional pastoral role has been superseded in large part in these situations, with much of the regular pastoral role being performed by a range of associate pastors/elders with a primary function as pastors, with little if any preaching component.

In the past, many churches did not have any pastoral assistance, and often the pastor was assisted by deacons, performing *de facto* pastoral roles, whilst also performing the normal administrative functions usually ascribed to deacons.

This has meant that often the expectancy of performing this *de facto* pastoral role, has led to a more selective process for choosing deacons, often precluding some well-equipped and gifted men from a serving ministry because they did not simultaneously qualify as elders.

We look at the pastoral role generally, but with a view to multiplying this role in order to meet the needs of growing congregations through the **introduction of elders**. Some practical considerations are given for the transition to introduce these changes.

Alongside this, what is the function of women in leadership ministries of the church?

* * * * *

**Available at the website: www.integritypublications.biz

TOWARD HEAVEN
THE ULTIMATE REALITY

DAVID A SWINCER

TOWARD HEAVEN:
THE ULTIMATE REALITY

Generally "Heaven" is treated with somewhat glib throwaway comments. Grandma died and went to heaven. There is almost a universal expectancy that everyone will get "there', whatever the form might be, with 70 virgins as a reward, the cheap culmination of a perverse life, through to the climactic and glorious hope of sincere Christians.

This book attempts to give perspectives and parameters that make the expectancy real and meaningful.

Uniquely, the whole panorama of earth's creation from beginning to end, is the framework. The eternal God is from everlasting to everlasting, and somehow in the middle of this continuum is a defined period of "this world order".

It is argued, that the perfection (heaven) that existed from all eternity prior to "this world order", must be restored after "this world order", and that Heaven is the Ultimate Reality that is the restoration after this world has been culminated in The New Heaven and the New Earth.

The remarkable difference in the two perfections—both before and after "this world order"—is that the future perfection, Heaven: The Ultimate Reality has a physical component that was not present in the perfection "from everlasting".

* * * * *

**Available at the website:
www.integritypublications.biz

PRAYER: PREMISED ON WORSHIP

Having been told to sacrifice his one-and-only son—who he had waited for 25 years to arrive, God told Abraham to sacrifice the lad to Him. No explanation.

And the Covenant God made to Abraham depended on that son. But Abraham was strong in faith—being persuaded of God—knowing that God had it all under control.

Abraham responded with implicit trust and obedience, and even though he was about 120 years old, he immediately proceeded into the desert to obey God.

On approaching the mountain for the sacrifice, he explained to his servants who accompanied him and Isaac:

> [5]... *"Stay here with the donkey while I and the boy go over there. We will WORSHIP and then we will come back to you."*
>
> Genesis 22:5.

Abraham wished to "appreciate God for His own sake". And his willingness to **worship**—no pipe organ or hymns—underlines the nature of **true worship** as it is addressed in this book. And hence the definition:

Worship is:

1. **an appreciation of God for His Own sake,**
2. **without regard to the circumstances,**
3. **without regard to any benefits that we might derive from Him, and**
4. **it is 24/7.**

This teaching is a must for every pastor, in their leadership of their flocks, as well as in their private devotions—as well as for every lay person.

SEE MORE BELOW:

CALVINISM REVISITED

In seeking to promote and support the Calvinist position, Benjamin Warfield sought to champion the cause by making some rather extravagant statements:

> He who believes in God without reserve and is determined *[free will!??]* that God shall be God to him, in all his thinking, feeling, willing - in the entire compass of his life activities, intellectual, moral, spiritual - throughout all his individual, social, religious relations - is, by the force of that strictest of all logic which presides over the outworking of principles into thought and life, by the very necessity of the case, a Calvinist.
>
> Warfield n.d., 13.

This can only be described as a ridiculously elitist statement. To believe in God in the terms described, does not even remotely require a person to be a Calvinist. Likewise, the following quote is equally elitist in the extreme.

> Religion (sic) in its substance is a sense of absolute dependence on God and reaches the height of its conception only when this sense of absolute dependence is complete and all pervasive, in the thought and feeling and life. But when this stage is reached we have just Calvinism.
>
> Warfield n.d., 21.

Sadly this statement is arrogant nonsense! Is this position—absolute dependence on God, etc.—not true of EVERY Christian? It is this arrogant approach that raises a serious concern of an elite theology above the Scriptures.

Such statements demand that a corrective be given, and hence this book.

**Available at the website:
www.integritypublications.biz

* * * * *

THE WILL OF GOD:

- *GOOD*
- *ACCEPTABLE*
  & ALWAYS
- *PERFECT*

DAVID A SWINCER

THE WILL OF GOD: GOOD AND ACCEPTABLE AND ALWAYS PERFECT

The title of this book is an expression of the following:

*¹Therefore, I urge you, brothers and sisters, in view of God's mercy, to **offer your bodies as a living sacrifice**, holy and pleasing to God—this is **your true and proper worship**. ²Do not conform to the pattern of this world, but be transformed by the renewing of your mind. **Then you will be able to test and approve what God's will is—his good, pleasing (acceptable) and perfect will.***

Romans 12:1-2, emphases added.

The question that is paramount, is, "How do we discover this **good and acceptable and perfect will?**"

*And **let the peace** (soul harmony which comes) from the Christ rule (**act as umpire continually**) in your hearts - **deciding and settling with finality** all questions that arise in your minds ...*

Colossians 3:15 (Amplified), emphases added.

This verse expresses in a quite convincing way, the last word on discovering the will of God: *Let the peace of God continually act as umpire in your hearts, **deciding and settling with finality** all questions that arise in your minds* (Colossians 3:15, adapted).

But this is not a privilege for anyone, as if it were some semi-magic trick to discover God's will. It is premised upon a deep and meaningful personal relationship with Christ. That relationship is the result of the conversion experience, and results in a life of growing into Christ's likeness—the process of sanctification. The expression of that life is then found in true Christian worship, with its commitment to God and the desire to live in obedience to Him—doing His will.

That is the theme of this book.

ISRAEL: APPLE OF GOD'S EYE

The first Jew was a Gentile. Prior to Abraham, there were no Jews—there was no nation of Israel.

Israel exists by the sovereign choice, plan, and action of God—the sovereign ruler of the universe. It deserves to be carefully acknowledged and recognised because of that origin—and more.

No other nation has ever attracted the detailed care, protection, and specific purpose as has Israel.

Through the Abrahamic Covenant, Israel was to become:
1. A great nation, deriving from Abraham. This was a personal blessing.
2. They would be given a land to possess—the land of Canaan. Beware of trifling with God's determination here.

Through the descendants of Abraham, down to Christ, there would be an international blessing. This belated nation would become central to God's purpose in order to determine the salvation destiny of the whole world.

God warned:

> ^{3}*I will bless those who bless you,*
> *and whoever curses you I will curse;*
>
> Genesis 12:3.

Nations that have failed to appreciate that statement, have learned to their own detriment., if they have tried to oppose Israel: they are opposing Israel's God.

Nations who have supported Israel, have benefited from the blessing of Israel's God.

Don't mess with Israel! They are the Apple of God's Eye!

* * * * *

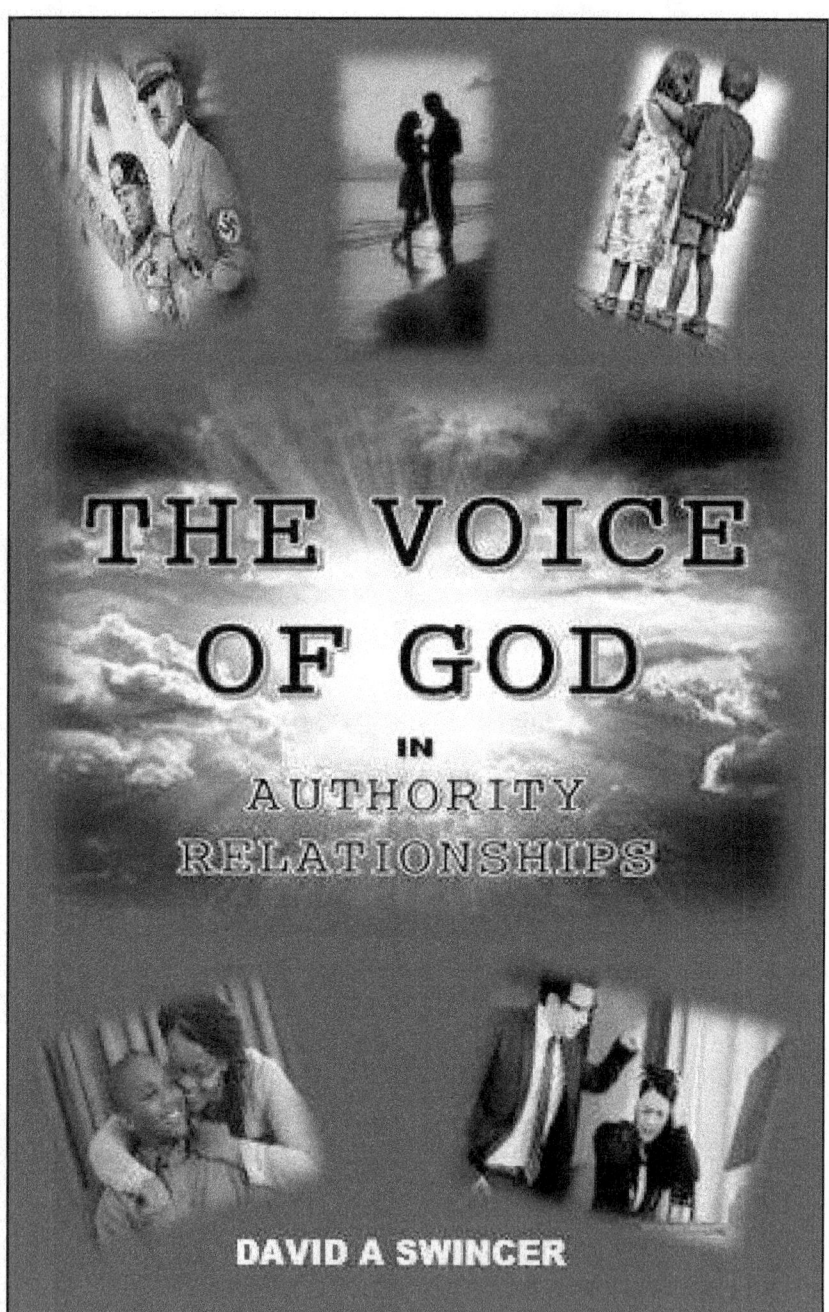

THE VOICE OF GOD
IN AUTHORITY RELATIONSHIPS

We live in a day when God's Voice is heard less and less. References to God or celebrations—like Christmas and Easter—are devalued and avoided, or reinterpreted for secular reasons.

References to God by prayers in Parliament and schools are reduced or removed. Loud, unprincipled voices are being heard instead of the truly authoritative Voice of God.

Against all this ignorance, we note that the only true source of authority is this same Almighty God Who is being silenced by the secular society. And the effects of this fact are being felt at all levels of society with exceptionally sad oppression and injustice.

All authority as expressed in the *functional* structures of our society—whether government and civil, employment and education, or domestic and private—is only ever *derived authority*. No one has authority vested in them by intrinsic right, or by self-achievement.

The only ones who claim such authority are dictators, petty tyrants, bully bosses, tyrannical husbands, intolerant drill instructors, etc. No one serving under them would ever mistake their voice as even remotely expressing the Voice of the true God.

The one-and-only true and sovereign God, Who alone possess authority, is loving, caring, compassionate, patient, just, longsuffering, instructive. How can this God's character be conveyed to our society? Only through the derived authority expressed by Christians in the functional structures of society. Others who have imbibed the Judeo-Christian ethic, will no doubt also express from their background, something of God's character as well.

The need of the hour, is for The Voice of God to be heard at all levels of society.

*****